"The heart of the leader is the soul of the organization, as Schneider paints a passionate picture of bringing your heart to the corner office. The heartbeat of an organization comes from the leader within you. Schneider crafts an excellent model to bring passion and heart to your work every day."

Dr. Carrie Buck
President, Pinecrest Foundation

Printed in the United States of America
First Printing, 2020

ISBN 978-0-9882727-4-3

Library of Congress Number: PENDING

US Copyright 1-8852391051 (Provisional)

Published by: Aegis Learning LLC

2225 Mundare Drive
Henderson, NV 89002

www.discoverAegis.com
info@discoverAegis.com

Ordering Information:
Quantity sales. Special discounts are available on quantity purchases by
wholesalers, corporations, associations, and others. For details, contact the
publisher at the email address above.

Edited by: Heidi Martin
Forward by: Robert Rippee

Disclaimer:
This book is presented solely for educational and personal development purposes.
The author and publisher are not offering it as legal, accounting, medical, or other
professional services advice. While best efforts have been used in preparing this
book, the author and publisher make no representations or warranties of any kind
and assume no liabilities of any kind with respect to the accuracy or completeness of
the contents and specifically disclaim any implied warranties of merchantability or
fitness of use for a particular purpose. Neither the author nor the publisher shall be
held liable or responsible to any person or entity with respect to any loss or incidental
or consequential damages caused, or alleged to have been caused, directly or
indirectly, by the information or programs contained herein. No warranty may be
created or extended by sales representatives or written sales materials. Every
company is different, and the advice and strategies contained herein may not be
suitable for your situation. You should seek the services of a competent professional
before beginning any improvement program. The story and its characters and entities
are fictional. Any likeness to actual persons, either living or dead, is strictly
coincidental.

"When there is no enemy within, the enemies outside cannot hurt you."

African Proverb

Contents   **Page**

Fun
Removing Judgement and Blame
Intention Setting
Mindfulness
Grieve, Cry and Move On
Purpose
Relationships

With Deeply Rooted Gratitude

In the process of writing this book, I found the love of my life. My unyielding thanks and appreciation to Lynn Jacquart for showing up at the perfect time. I love you. I will always love you and I look forward to our life together.

The team at Aegis Learning continue to be incredibly supportive and encouraging of our vision and mission to help people and organizations succeed. I am deeply grateful for their loyalty, dedication, and focus.

Thank you to the many friends and family members that rallied to support me during the transitions of early 2017. The outpouring of encouragement and friendship was unlike anything I had ever experienced and will never be forgotten.

And certainly not least, the love of a loyal companion can never be underestimated or unappreciated. Sydney Marie, my Pembroke Welsh Corgi companion has never left my side or failed to remind me of what is important and what is not.

Forward

By Robert Rippee

I believe it was sometime in early 2012 when I first met Tim Schneider. I was a senior executive for a large company in Las Vegas, and Tim's firm was conducting a leadership assessment and training program for the company. I went back into my photo library and found some images from that morning; I recall it vividly. At that time, I was relatively new to the company, and this was one of the first development sessions for my team. To this day, I am thankful for that fateful training session. What appeared to be an essential but somewhat routine professional development session would result in the building of friendship, mentorship, and respect with an expert in the leadership domain and something else. Throughout my tenure at that company, Tim became my feedback partner. Initially, I credited the healthy relationship to trust formed by a common background. As it turned out, both Tim and I went to the same University for undergraduate studies, although the point is still open for debate if we crossed paths during those cowboy years. Perhaps the best evidence of that common background was the immediate authenticity we expressed to each other. As Tim says so well, authenticity has become the buzzword of the current decade, but it was natural for Tim and me. If I recall correctly, upon discovery of this shared lineage, the first reference was to a famous local watering hole. We connected, and it was indeed authentic.

As I read Tim's manuscript, I was astounded by the convergence of his thoughtful and well-researched factors with events and people from my experience. It is as if Tim can reach back into the memory bank of our professional and personal experiences and touch on those moments. In some cases, providing us with an explanation or a renewed understanding of why those situations turned out the way they did. In other cases, helped us to answer, how could or how should I have handled that differently? From that self-reflection, Tim crafts a practical guide to dealing with future situations and giving the reader insights into how their lives can be changed. Changed so that future conditions have the potential to be handled differently, changed if you will, long before they happen. And along the way, gain a greater insight into the relationship between your own emotions and behaviors.

A Heart for Leadership is not so much of a study of leadership principles as it is a simple to follow a set of instructions to consciously understand the relationship between emotions and behavior. This is the foundation of the methodology Tim presents. It is to understand how self-awareness of this relationship can support more effective leadership practices by using that one superpower we all share, being human. We are emotional beings, and often those emotions seem to act on their own. Through self-reflection and practice, a leader can reign in the bucking bronco and turn it into a confident and calm companion.

Tim presents a toolkit for this process in the last section, Changing – The Tools for Change. This section is truly the most potent and compelling section of the book. In that unique, approachable Tim Schneider style, he takes the reader on a journey of self-discovery. And while I feel a great deal of Tim's journey provided the roadmap for this process, it nonetheless provides the reader with a digestible and doable path to change. Lasting change, the kind of change that can add a new dimension to a leadership role, a human dimension. And as Tim says, bring enhanced effectiveness as a leader and increase your happiness and satisfaction.

From my perspective, this is leadership mastery, and Tim will show you how. Tim is building a theory of motivation and behavior here, along with the methodical prescription for understanding and mastering it. Beginning with developing the benefits of this inward focus through self-care and time investment, Tim enables that inward focus to become part of a deeper self-understanding through the practice of journaling, meditation, and a feedback partner. This section is a non-stop read because, without these wonderful tools, the final factors are difficult, if not impossible. It is within these last sections that I feel Tim's journey resonating through the pages. Gratitude, forgiveness, giving, fun are the waypoints of Tim's life. Yet they are the waypoints of my life as well. This is the illuminating culmination of his book, a self-discovery of what was in you the whole time – a purpose. And if one extends that purpose beyond our relationships, we see that purpose enacted in professional settings. But something different this time, a conscious and deliberate heartfelt driven leadership.

Tim is a gifted writer, a wonderful mentor, and an extraordinary man. While I assume his personal journal includes doodles of fishing in the mountains, I am confident it also consists of looking into the heart of a man. A man who used his self-reflection to the benefit of others. That, dear reader, is a heart for leadership.

Robert Rippee, MBA, Ph.D. candidate is the Director, Hospitality Innovation Lab and esports Lab at the International Gaming Institute of UNLV. He is also the CEO and co-founder of RM Labs LLC and chief consultant for Elysian LLC. Robert was a commissioned officer and pilot for the United States Navy.

Welcome

"Do your work with your whole heart and you will succeed. There's so little competition."

Elbert Hubbard

I'm inviting you on a journey. There are times it will not be easy. There are times that you may want to give up. But the one thing I can assure you is that your journey will be worth it.

This is not a path to enlightenment. I'm not even sure what that is and the people who claim to be enlightened aren't very much fun to be around.

This is also not a path to God. That is on you.

This is a journey to a better, happier, healthier, more effective you.

Of my three books on leadership, none has been a more passionate pursuit than this one. Passionate because of knowing the power of unlocking the heart and what it means for success and passionate because of the personal journey that it took to get to this point.

For the last 25 years, I have had the sincere honor and privilege of watching tens of thousands of people grow and build the skills needed for leadership success. It has been a constant career love affair with these people and their growth and development. The **Ten Competencies of Outstanding Leadership** model has proven to deliver remarkable results in people and companies across the globe.

To a point.

It wasn't until about three years ago that I discovered the value of healthy emotional composition and the power of the heart. Up until then, I always believed that the mastery of skills and competencies would drive success in leadership but sadly, alone, they will not. A leader must have a heart. A healthy heart. A heart that drives attitudes and beliefs, which in turn create, sustained behaviors.

When healthy and positive emotional composition and heart combine with the proven competencies, a leader, or any person, becomes unstoppable in their ability to succeed and an unyielding source of good in every situation.

Another strong motivator in producing this book and the associated work was my initial frustration with finding usable information about becoming heart strong and attitude positive. What I did find was a bunch of "you must dig deep into yourself", "you have to become mindful", "you need to heal your heart" and "you have to really understand you and be authentic".

Awesome! But how?

The resources for how were rare. Even getting to the root of phrases and definitions were tough. Many people used the words and tossed them as if pennies to a fountain, but few were willing to explain the meaning and application of the words. Even though my heart is in a great spot, I may harm the next human that says, "You need to get in touch with yourself".

The final piece of motivation for **A Heart for Leadership** was to connect the learning, steps, and other pieces of emotional intelligence to a business and working setting. There will be no turbans, yoga mats or funky rituals here (and for the record, I have nothing against those, and I have several friends who get that deep into spiritualism). You will not need to renounce your religion or go to a mountaintop. I targeted producing a practice for you to unleash the power of your heart into the world.

Again, with great gratitude and acknowledgment of blessing, I have had the privilege and honor of using the steps and techniques in this book to coach people and the results have been amazing. Leaders who start out with good skills but have such darkness, bitterness, resentment, and anger in their heart have blossomed into truly outstanding leaders and even better people. Watching this unfold, hearing from them, hearing from their team members and families has validated this approach many times over.

One final opening note: I like lists. They speak to my logical and OCD side. They are neat. So be forewarned, you will see many lists.

When and How

"Curiosity keeps leading us down new paths."

Walt Disney

This book is designed to provide key narratives for your growth and a calendared approach to unlocking your heart power. The journey will take us through a couple of months and there is no perfect way to do this. Some of you will take a little longer. Some move through multiple steps in a single day. Some will start, stop, and start again. All of that is okay.

The practices, habits and reflections in this book work and they work well but just like barbeque, everyone has their own secret ingredients, temperature settings and approach.

Look for sections in the book titled **The Journey** for the daily guidance interspersed throughout.

Why Unlock Your Heart

"The power of the heart is the power of life."

Gary Zukov

Most of the benefit of unlocking your heart will come out throughout the book and very organically. You will discover benefits beyond your wildest dreams and capacity for life that you never knew existed.

As we become more mindful, more in touch with who we really are and combine our emotional composition and heart with our skills, we will see:

1. More closely and deeply connected relationships. Your influence will grow and so will your care for others.

2. Improvement in your ability to provide genuine empathy. Team members greatly admire this trait in their leaders.

3. Enhanced patience and openness to different approaches.

4. Dramatically reduced stress and anxiety levels. This will improve your leadership quality as well as your total life.

5. Much better focus on what is important and the ability abandon what is not meaningful. There is not a leader or successful person alive that does not want this outcome.

6. Greater approachability and information flow coming to us.

7. Higher levels of physical energy. It takes energy to be a leader and this will get that spring back in your step.

8. Your decisions and choices will be better and delivered under less duress and you will engage the ability to see unintended consequences and casualty.

I really wanted to lead with this little part, but the better angels of my nature kept this in abeyance. There is so much stigma associated with mindfulness, using our heart and being genuine. Those stigmas are pervasive with many leaders and tend to have a generational bias. So, to quell those stigmas, what won't happen to you is:

1. You will not become soft and weak. You will find and use strength that you never knew you had but it will be less demonstrative, less assaultive, less abrasive, and easier to digest by those around you.

2. You will not lose focus on your vision and strategic planning. Some schools of mindful practice teach a "let it happen" or a "let it come to you" model. We are leaders and we will continue to keep an eye towards the future, drive results and be mindful at the same time.

3. You will not stop holding people accountable. As indicated in item #1 above, the method and style may improve but your adherence to standards will not diminish.

Encouragement

"Fall seven times, stand up eight."

Japanese Proverb

My highest encouragement for you is to try this. A real, legitimate, focused effort try.

Many of us, and certainly including me, develop a false sense of success and happiness that produces a complacency in our growth. We view ourselves as happy and successful without looking at what could be. This comfortable complacency is our biggest enemy as a leader and person because we are now sleepwalking until something shakes us out of it.

Another point of encouragement is that many of us, me included, don't really have a good understanding of who we really are and what we are about. We have crafted a narrative about ourselves and use that as our self-awareness. Sadly, our little narrative is not close to the reality of who we are, and what is at our core.

Again, please try this and see what your results look like. Risk some time investment and doing some things differently, and even uncomfortable for a more successful, happy, and productive you. By power of statistics, the chances are overwhelmingly good that it will have a profound impact on your life and career.

The Trinity of Leadership Success

"A good head and a good heart are always a formidable combination."

Nelson Mandela

One of the first questions that is often asked is why. Why does heart matter? What difference does my heart make if I am using the right skills and competencies and achieving a certain level of success?

And those are very fair questions.

Leadership begins within, is fueled by your use of proven competencies, and is supported by the environment in which you work.

The heart of a leader completes the trinity of leadership success, potential and full actualization of ability. Consider three circles. The first circle contains your competencies and skills. The most important of those competencies include communication, team member engagement, coaching, self-mastery, and empowerment. Also, among them are decision-making, innovation and change, strategic planning, relationships and external management, and courage and risk. Within each competency, there are critical skills to master as well. These competencies and supporting skills, when mastered and used consistently will lead you to a tremendous level of success just on their own.

Developing the use of competencies and skills is a cognitive or thinking processed piece of learning. It is developed through the engagement of intellectual capacity and stored in process, mind memory. The learning occurs from reading, seeing, doing, and is reinforced by the successes associated with the application of those skills. Your mind and memory drive the use of competencies and skills when not combined with other elements of success.

The second circle is the environment in which you operate. No successful person or leader can truly actualize his or her abilities and talents without a supporting and supportive environment. Within this circle, are the organizational and environmental competencies of providing opportunity, valuing people, providing of needs, creating opportunity for growth, and providing feedback to people. This type of environment will allow leaders to fully utilize in a supporting climate, their abilities, and talents. Together with competencies, this creates a powerful combination for potential success.

But wait. That's not all.

The third circle becomes the final driving piece of personal and leadership success. It is within that circle that the power of your emotions, heart and beliefs can be managed and unleashed. The heart, soul and emotional composition of a leader will drive beliefs which, in-turn, drive actions and behaviors. This can be viewed in a variety of ways including another circular view of your emotions and heart, which are at the core of who you are. Your beliefs are driven by that emotional composition and your emotions then create the reality of behaviors and application of skills in all situations.

In the simplest of analogies, if you are upset, then your attitude reflects that. Your outward behaviors will become a projection of that attitude and belief set.

Conversely, if you are happy, then your beliefs and attitude will be upbeat and positive. The outward behaviors driven by this will be much more positive in nature. You will smile, you will encourage, you will provide positive feedback, but only if your heart is in the right place.

Another superpower associated with leadership heart is the ability to drive sustained positive competencies and skills. Quite bluntly, anyone can memorize a skill or change a habit temporarily. We all do that. To sustain long-term desired behaviors, alignment with attitudes and belief and ultimately, emotional composition and heart must occur.

Consider for a moment that we could all quickly learn scales and a simple tune on a piano. All of that is cognitive learning and we will have this knocked down in 15 minutes. However, to continue to play that music, expand the selection, execute with passion, and achieve great musical results, your heart must be into it and belief in the outcome must be present. Without those, the song will sound mechanical and interest will quickly wane.

With alignment of heart, attitude and actions, any leader and any person become unstoppable.

Symptoms Indicating a Need to Unlock Heart

"The only thing greater than the power of the mind is the courage of the heart."

John Nash

Our world gives us plenty of clues when it is necessary and time to work on unlocking emotional and heart power. Some of those clues are right-between-the-eyes blunt force and some are a bit more subtle. Examine these, see where you are at, and see if there is indeed work to be done to unlock your heart:

- Stuck in a low-level motivation (more on that later in this section)

- Operating from fears (more on that as well)

- Anxiety and edginess

- Frequent use of sarcasm or snarky comments

- Need to be the center of attention often or always

- Lack of focus or persistence with tasks and projects

- Lack of physical energy or a drained feeling

- Avoidance of conflict

- Strained relationships at work or in your personal life

- Procrastination and avoidance

- Reluctance to or fighting of change

- Inability to sustain the use of new skills or approaches

- Low general demeanor or surliness towards work and people at work

- Stressed out

- Negativity and pessimism for the future

- Poor, snappy, or edgy verbal tone

- Dour and sour facial expressions

- Lack of genuine human empathy

- Overly judgmental of others

- Isolation from others or activities you enjoy

- Blaming others for challenges and failures

- Reliance on drugs or alcohol to escape

There is also a need to look at the recurring patterns in your life. Things like these point to a need to tap into the energy of your heart and emotions:

- Repeated failures in business or bouncing from one career path to another frequently

- Easily disenfranchised with organizations and people

- Novelty of new things wears off quickly

- Complaints from team members that have similar themes

- Trying to change others to adapt to you

- Trail of relationship casualty and failed interpersonal relationships

None of these is devastating by themselves and we all certainly spend time in these spots from time to time. The one thing to watch for is frequent occurrences of these symptoms, and how long they last. When they occur regularly, it is time to unlock the power of your heart.

Motivationally Stuck

Dr. Abraham Maslow's groundbreaking and baseline work on human motivation describes five levels of needs. This Hierarchy of Needs demonstrates that lower level needs must be satisfied first before higher tier needs may be met. As a person moves up the pyramid of needs, their motivation increases until they reach self-actualization. This stage is the highest level of motivation and all lower level needs - physiological, security, social, and self-esteem - are met. Quite simply, the more needs that are being met, the higher the motivation until the pinnacle is achieved.

So, what happens when someone is stuck in a lower
level and plateaus? Their motivation levels cap off at
that level as well. Think of this example:

> A person is constantly straining against their
> resources to make ends meet. There is
> consistent worry and pessimism about the ability
> to pay bills and ever live in abundance or have
> discretionary spending ability.

In this example, being motivationally stuck in physiological needs will have a dramatic impact on this person's ability to achieve more in life. When constantly worrying about money, opportunity will be passed by, relationships will be strained, self-esteem will suffer, and the heart of this person will become tainted on money. Their brain will follow suit and this person will openly obsess about money, accumulation of things, and savings.

One example that we tend to hear a great deal in organizations related to being stuck on security needs:

> Someone is always talking about the number of years until the retirement account will pay them what they think they need to survive in their senior years. Rather than looking forward to being able to make a difference, they are counting down to when the retirement savings will allow them some mystical security.

This stuck point can be devastating to effectiveness and has a significant adverse impact on motivations and the desire to change, move forward and thrive. This motivational stuck is all about just surviving another day, week, month, or year.

Another example that becomes common:

> The person that cannot do anything alone or be alone for more than two seconds. There is constant insecurity about people and a need to be connected to someone or groups of people all the time.

This example points to a deeply unmet social need (Maslow's third tier) and by not being comfortable alone, they will never be able to achieve comfort with others and truly meaningful relationships.

Looking for Stuck Points

We all get stuck momentarily and there is certainly nothing wrong with a twice a month fretting a bit about where paychecks went or spending a bit of time being lonely or even wondering about what the future may bring. These are all normal little stops for our brain and emotional composition.

Where motivational stuck becomes dangerous is when we spend a bunch of our time and energy there. Look at and get feedback about what you talk about or even obsess about. Really think about where you are motivationally and strive always to seek the next level on the pyramid.

What is Showing Up?

"What you resist persists."

Rick Warren

There is one more quick self-check to see if your heart needs to be unlocked. It is quick, but complicated to get our heads around.

Look at and spend some time thinking about what is showing up in your life. Is it really what you want and desire, or are there elements of dissatisfaction or evenly some deeply rooted pieces where you are not living as you desire?

To be specific, examine who is in your life. Are you pulling great people around you or are you a bug light for toxic and negative humans? Are the relationships you have mutually supportive and caring or is it one way only? These are tough questions but are necessary as you move forward to unlock your emotional power.

Take a moment and reflect on your last three or four thoughts. Were they positive, upbeat, and encouraging or were they dark and negative? What is the ratio of good thoughts to negative or bad thoughts? This one is a good sign that there are some unresolved issues blocking the emotions that drive your thought patterns.

Another specific view is about obstacles you are facing. Have you done everything right in an area, but the results are not coming? Are you working extremely hard and have truly little to show for it? Have you been passed over for a promotion? Have you been turned down for a loan needed to go into business for yourself? Are you wondering what is holding you back and preventing that success?

Whether consciously known to you or not, answers of yes to the above reveal some unresolved issues you are carrying in your heart and emotional composition. Most common among those are:

- Unrepaired relationships

- Un-grieved loss

- Motivations for your actions that are not rooted in good intention

- Projections to the world that are not what you want or hope (negative perceptions by others)

Have you ever watched news accounts of crime victims reaching out and connecting with the perpetrators of their pain? Although grotesque to think about, these are perfect examples of why relationships, even the most fleeting, need to have some closure, questions answered and some point of clearing.

Unrepaired relationships pull consciously and subconsciously on all of us. Blocking someone out of your life is not repair and simply serves to bury the hurt and block deeper into our subconscious, making it harder to heal. As we all suffer disconnect with others, the heart healthy works to repair while the emotionally unpowered seek to bury the disconnect and simply forget. Quick little note here - you will not really forget. It may move away from the top of your mind but never out of your subconscious thoughts and emotional composition. As we move through the tools and practices in this book, you will have a pathway to repair these relationships - or at minimum - attempt to repair them. We will not sugarcoat this area in any form. This is difficult and some relationships have decades of estrangement.

Another hard examination are the un-grieved losses in our lives. Very personally, this one weighed on me for many years and there are still a couple of losses that need some grieving time. It was not until years after I lost my dad and mom, did I fully mourn their loss and clear that heart blockage. There is a likelihood that you too are carrying some un-grieved losses in your life. They do not need to be a death and could come in the form of a lost marriage, failed business or even a missed opportunity.

Similar to relationships, our losses cannot simply be buried, and we cannot rely on time to heal these wounds. Time blunts some of the pain. However, the loss still remains in our hearts and subconscious minds and creates blocks to our success and our ability to capitalize on our heart and emotional power. It will become a matter of finding, acknowledging, and then finally grieving those losses to move on successfully.

Your motivations and projections will be examined in detail later in this book. However, it suffices to say that they drive a big part of our emotional health and heart power. When motives are pure and positive, those types of results will follow. When motives are less than pure, the results that show up in your life will reflect that as well.

Projections are the same. You will attract exactly what you project. Think about this equation for a moment. You attract what you project. At work and in life.

The unhealthy elements (and people) in our lives appear because of something we have projected to the world. We certainly do not mean to do that, but there is something buried in our emotional composition that keeps driving our projected behaviors. It could be incredibly old, or something deeply rooted in a difficult experience. Only you know and it is up to you to find out about it.

The Model to Heart and Emotional Power

"Simplicity is the ultimate sophistication."

Leonardo Da Vinci

The path to overcoming heart stuck and unleashing the incredible power of your emotions is quite simple. Not easy, but simple in design.

Knowing

Not the kind of "know yourself deeply" with no instructions, but rather the kind of progressive and meaningful self-awareness that provides the insight to move forward. We cannot fix or tune what we don't know may not be functioning at its highest capacity.

<u>Changing</u>

There are a set of tools, practices, and skills - helpers if you will - that create the baseline for us to move forward. None of them is difficult, but they do require a disciplined and consistent approach.

This set of highly validated best practices will unlock and grow your emotional composition, power of your heart, and create the space for success in your life.

Knowing yourself is the Starting Point

"What is necessary to change a person is to change his awareness of himself."

Abraham Maslow

The incorporation of heavy doses of self-awareness followed by changes in thoughts and emotional composition has produced lasting and sustained impact in the competencies and skills needed for success. More simply, thoughts and emotions drive action. Action creates results and success. Actions and behaviors can be modified in a short time frame, but long-term change comes when core parts of you make a move towards the better. Personal awareness and understanding are also the starting point for greater mindfulness, enhanced effectiveness as a leader and your own happiness and satisfaction. This series is going to be devoted to the natural first step in making those long-term changes and that is to understand yourself on a deep and core level. It is only then, that you can redirect some things in your life to achieve greater and more desired results.

A huge reason in committing these practices to this book is that we have seen other coaches talk about self-awareness without providing the tools to really unlock this power. To say know yourself is not nearly enough. A road map of how to do it in a significant and meaningful way is needed. Without that, the command to be self-aware can be frustrating and meaningless.

There are challenges associated with knowing ourselves, our true selves. First and most formidable is the critical concept that you are not the expert in you. That is right; you do not know yourself nearly as well as you think you do.

In fact, most people create a narrative that is perpetually reinforced through self-talk. This narrative has little connection to the truth but rather paints a picture to what we would like to be or what we would like others to see in us. We need to silence this voice and narrative so we can find out who we really are and discover those areas that are limiting our potential and growth.

The next challenge to good self-awareness is to find a truth teller for your life. A truth teller or feedback partner can be anyone, but they must have the ability to tell you the absolute truth about you without any fear of retaliation. They must also feel safe in providing you the feedback you need and will come to crave. This person also cannot have ulterior motives or a hidden agenda in providing you with feedback and must do so from a position of care, compassion, and love for you. They will become your partner in growth and change.

Because of the way they love us, a spouse or significant other is generally not a good feedback partner or truth teller. There will always be something they hold back on or lessen to protect our feelings. Feedback partners are a gift from God and the universe. If you do not have one, please find one. If you have one, treat that relationship like solid gold.

The care and feeding of your truth teller or feedback partner is extremely important and the process to obtain feedback from this source matters greatly. Try this method to get the best quality information from a feedback source:

1. Frame the Conversation – Tell the other person - your feedback partner - that you need a little feedback about a situation or area of concern for you.

2. Make it Safe – Reiterate to your feedback partner that you want the best information and the truth.

3. Ask Direct Questions – Questions phrased in a manner of "Do I (whatever behaviors you're interested in)?" or "Have you seen/heard me (some behavior)?"

4. Ask Open Ended Questions – Asking about how you sound, how you come across to others or how you are perceived are powerful sources of self-awareness information.

5. Remain Open – Not every piece of feedback you receive, even from a trusted source and long-time feedback partner, is going to be perfectly accurate and true. No one can see into your heart, but everyone can observe and evaluate your behaviors. Even if you don't believe a piece of feedback to be accurate, before responding back with the automatic "I don't do that" or the equally

pervasive "I don't see that" .... Spend some time processing the feedback and see if it is possible that some of your behavioral projects lead someone to that conclusion or see how it could be a perception that someone carries about you.

6. Appreciate the Feedback – Even the difficult and not-enjoyable parts. Say thank you and nothing else. Don't push back. Don't ask for examples. Don't put any burden on a feedback provider because you will risk them providing feedback to you in the future.

The final challenge of growing self-awareness is data-driven information about you. Assessments tools and evaluations can be a great source of actionable self-awareness when used properly and openly. We use the family of DiSC assessment tools to yield critical information about motivations, desired environment, relationship values, communication style and much more. One of the powerful findings in the DiSC assessment and in many other similar tools is behavioral blind spots.

There are those behaviors that are known to you, and those known to everyone else. There are those behaviors that are known to you and unknown to everyone else. Those are your private behaviors. In addition, there are behaviors that are known to everyone around you, but you are completely blind to them. Those are your behavioral blind spots. Everyone, except you, see them with crystal clarity. Some common examples include your verbal tone, overly high expectations of others, conveyance of praise (many people think they give more than they really do), facial expressions, patience with others and adding too much value (talking and adding when it's not needed and adds nothing).

Especially for leaders, blind spots must be identified and managed because they can have an adverse impact on self-awareness, relationships with others and your credibility as a leader. The only known cure for blind spots is through the awareness provided by a feedback partner and assessment data.

Not all assessments are created equally. Make sure you are using a bona fide and validated psychometric tool. DiSC, MBTI (Myers-Briggs) and Preference Index are examples of good tools that can provide great self-awareness information. "What Stars Wars Character

Am I?" and puzzles to find the 9 in a sea of 8's are not valid and should be looked at for only the extremely limited entertainment value they provide.

The magic (it's scientific, empirically driven, and statistically accurate) that assessments have with blind spots is that all of them will have some descriptions and language you do not agree with. You read it, deny the existence of that characteristic, and boldly proclaim that this problem with these kinds of tests, they are never accurate. The funny thing is we accept the complimentary language in them quickly and willingly.

For me, this phenomenon played itself out long ago. There are many great descriptors in my DiSC assessment. Causes action, leads change, bold. I accepted those and wore them like a badge of honor. Also, a line said I could become manipulative and quarrelsome. Never! The nerve to say that. So grossly untrue!

I handed my DiSC assessment narrative to a trusted feedback source and asked her to read it. She did. I asked what she saw. Her response was "you". Further quizzing asked about the manipulative and quarrelsome line. She affirmed again it was totally me and cited examples of the same. It took me many months of reflection and self-reflection to accept this projection of mine and work hard to reduce it. It was a big blind spot.

Other sources of data-driven self-awareness can include reviews, performance appraisal and notes from team members or key stakeholders in your organization.

Now on to the areas of deeper awareness that will really unlock the true you. The coming sections will focus on the 'what' and how to of:

Awareness-Motivations

Understanding why you are doing something and if that motivation is consistent with core values and beliefs. Motivations can be solid and even pure, or they can be designed to hurt and harm. Many people mask their motivations or are unaware of them entirely.

Awareness-Your Influencers

Your inner circle of those that influence your emotions, beliefs and ultimately, your behavior are important. Understanding why people are connected to you and who you allow influence over you is a nice place of examination. This also relates closely to motivation, as you will now look at the motivations of others (warning: not all are good).

Awareness-Life Patterns

Short-term patterns are easy enough to spot and change. The more difficult challenge is to look at long-term recurring patterns and learn to replicate the awesome while eliminating the bad ones. Are there sustained pieces of success showing up for you that can be replicated? Are there patterns of failed marriages, businesses and relationships that need to be eliminated? Is there a pattern of sameness? All are either changeable or repeatable based on your desired outcome. Think for a minute about the people with multiple failed businesses or marriages that always blame someone else but not look at the long-term pattern for answers.

Awareness-Projections

Related to patterns, what you project to others has a considerable influence on the world around you and what you achieve. Your kids become the easiest example because of the degree of influence you have with them. Your team members are another. Project positive and successful things and that will be what occurs around you. Project dysfunction and sadly, that is what will return to you. Do not be shocked when your team (or kids) turn out exactly like you.

Awareness-Emotions

Your emotions drive your attitude and your attitude drives your behavior. That simple. A customer/friend asked me to help him with his verbal tone a few days ago. His issue is not his tone but the emotional composition driving his tone.

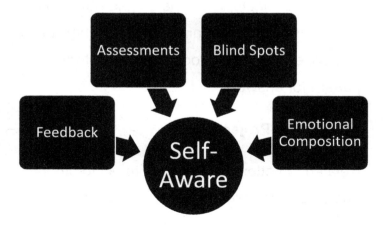

Motivations and Motives

"The moment there is suspicion about a person's motives, everything he does becomes tainted."

Mahatma Gandhi

Motivations and motives are a complex set of thoughts and emotions that drive significant parts of our behavior. When understood and correctly managed, this can lead to powerful changes in our lives and work. It is a great starting point for a significant upgrade to our self-awareness.

As with just about everything else in life, there are great motivations and motives and poor ones. The purpose of this section is to encourage the examination of what motives are driving your behaviors and responses.

Motive of Love and Enjoyment

The best motive of all is when love or pure unbridled enjoyment drives behaviors or responses. I have a buddy that loves baseball. He eats, sleeps, talks, and plays baseball. It is his point of love, enjoyment, and passion. Each time he talks about it, it is driven by his love for the game. Similarly, a parent's interaction with their child is often driven by a motive of love. Not to say that each interaction is enjoyable, but it is driven by the love of the best interest for that child. Love and enjoyment-based motivations will produce the best results, behaviors, and ultimate success. When this motive drives your behavior, it will be obvious to all around you through your displayed demeanor and projected energy. You will light up a room with this motivation.

Motive of Care and Assistance

My mind immediately recalls Mother Teresa when thinking about this motivation and motive set. No one more selfless and egoless in her pursuit of caring for others probably exited in modern times. This motivation has a dark and evil twin that will appear below and comes up a lot in discussions and work on becoming a giving person. This motive should be examined anytime you volunteer, donate, or offer care and assistance to others. Are you doing it to truly help or to shine favor upon yourself? Likewise, in the workplace, when assistance is offered without any strings attached or expectation of even appreciation, the motivation is coming from the right spot.

Motive of Support

Like care and assistance, support offered without judgment and any expectation is coming from a great spot. When that supporting ear turns judgmental, gossiping and used against someone, that motivation is now quite polluted.

Motive of Survival

Dr. Abraham Maslow taught the best and most lasting lessons related to this motive. The need to feed oneself trumps all other needs. Almost primitive in its view, it produces a 'me first' behavior and often leads to unethical actions or sacrificing people (and love/enjoyment motivations) for self-preservation. Although this motive must be present in some form, it should be subordinated for the greater good of a love or care for others motivation, with the understanding that basic needs will be provided when motives are aligned. This motive can become part of a company culture and sacrifice doing the right thing or superior customer service for survival motivations of layoffs or worse.

Motive of Attention

This motivation appears a great deal in social media and even takes the form of people playing the role of victim or even making up victim status (gentle reminder: you signed that 'bad' deal for the car with your eyes wide open and conscious). This motivation also appears many times under the guise of giving of support when the real motive is to draw personal attention to the act. Children are great models of this motive in both good and bad behavior and adults will often do something outrageous just for the attention value. There is sociological work being done right now about the incredible rise in people getting tattoos (yes, I have some too) and why they do it.

Motive of Embarrassment

The motive to embarrass and the need to be right (below) are very closely related. The embarrassment motive will often show up in sarcastic remarks and cutting-edge humor that is designed to make someone else embarrassed or feel badly. Look at the impact of your words and actions and use good reaction avoidance to cure this motivation.

Motive of Superiority

As with embarrassment, this motive has a winner and loser. Since social media as burst into our reality, this motivation has become significantly more public. A simple test on this motive is to reflect about why being right is so important. Great judgment will lead you to understand that being right is not nearly as important as allowing others to be right and to carefully choose the spots for being right carefully.

Motive of Revenge

The darkest of all the motives and one driven by pure fear is revenge. Like embarrassment as a motive but with deeper behavioral impact. When someone is driven by the motive of revenge, it becomes blinding and fear feeding to the point of losing rationality in thought and judgment. The behaviors driven by revenge are not always the highly open tire slashing variety. Many of the revenge motive driven behaviors are covert and include gossip, spreading lies and working to undermine the success of others.

None of us, certainly me included, can ever have total purity of motivations and driving motives. But what we can do is add some significant thought to why we are doing something and what our motives are behind them. When we know that the motives are solid, we should continue those behaviors. Conversely, when those motivations are not good or even dark, we need to step back and cease those behaviors and repair the damage when possible.

1. Review a couple of recent choices and decisions you made.

2. Identify the motivations for those decisions and choices. It can be one clear motivation or the combination of several.

3. Think about how people can question your motivations by looking at your choices.

4. Journal and note any time you can identify when your motives were not correctly aligned and good in purpose.

Your Influencers

"Close friends love you for who you are, not for what they want you to be."

Ted Rall

The people in our lives have tremendous power and influence with us. Their thoughts matter. Their opinions matter. Their approval matters.

Understanding how each of those people influence our choices, decisions and how we ultimately can live out our purpose is another powerful step on the road to real self-awareness. We hope the people closest to us and who have a high degree of influence over our choices have our best interests at heart but, sadly, that is not always the case. It is only through examination that we can see what our influencers have for motivations and desired outcomes for us and in turn, allow us to manage who we allow to influence our actions.

We have used this type of activity for years when working with one of the key leadership competencies, relationship power and external management, and it works extremely well for examining our influencers more closely.

The Core Influencers

Draw a dot or small circle at the center of a piece of paper. This is you. The highest degree of influence that should occur in your decisions, choices, actions, and behavior is you. You are or should be the center of your influence universe.

This is where you and I must learn to trust our own judgment, values, and choices. Stop being so anxious to share each choice and decision in your life with others seeking their approval or opinion. If it works for you, you feel right about it, it fits your core values and is congruent with your purpose - go with it. Other's opinions and what they would do is extremely less important than many of us think.

Over-solicitation of input is a sign of low self-esteem and projected in either a lack of confidence or a false bravado of courage. True trust of your own choices and decisions is quiet and does not seek lots of input nor require a puffing public proclamation.

Tier One

Next, draw a small circle outside of the 'you' dot or circle. This is your closest sphere of influencers and the people that you have allowed the strongest voice in your life. This population should be small. The more people you allow significant voice and influence, the greater confusion, second-guessing and poor choices you will make.

This little band must be beyond reproach. The motives of this group must be purely for your best interest, connect completely with your core values and understand your purpose and personal vision. Any doubt about a motive or the reason for the connection and that person does not belong in your inner circle of influence. This group will also be static over time as well and the members will not change much. Who was a trusted inner circle member ten years ago is likely to remain if you are correctly vetting these relationships.

Tiers Two and Three

The second layer of your relationships and relationship strength is where you may solicit some input over unimportant things and certainly not on life-altering matters. These people are not known well enough to understand their motives in offering you advice and they certainly do not know your purpose, passions, or core values much more than a cursory level. These people are friends, relatives, and business associates but not the deeply connected ones. Some individuals may have expertise in a certain area, but not universally to influence major choices of yours.

By the time you start looking at the third ring on your paper you are now looking mostly at acquaintances or those you are friendly with but not really friends. If you welcome influence from this population, you are doing nothing more than conducting a poll or shopping for an answer that you want to hear.

General Influencer Rules

When you really look deeply into the people you allow influence you need to make sure those people provide you with genuine truth and not just what they think you want to hear. People that share the good and bad in a forthright manner should have a permanent place as your influencer. Those that simply agree with you or don't call you on your crap should be shown a place in an outer circle.

Likewise, if an influencer is trying to curry favor or wants something from you, they have no real influencer value. Think about those people who offer hollow compliments related to appearance or those that come across too gushing about some achievement of yours. Nice - absolutely - but no value as an influencer.

The final general thought about an influencer is the most controversial. Many times, those personally closest (spouse, significant other, new boyfriend, parent) are not the best influencers because they lack the objectivity to be completely honest and their motives are tainted by their close relationship with you.

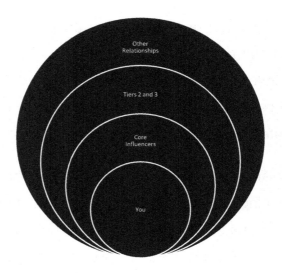

Take some time over the next few days and see who you allow high degrees of influence in your life and if they should be in that position. Nevertheless, most importantly, make sure the highest degree of influence always rests with you.

1. Examine those that you allow to have influence in your life, choices and decisions using a tiered circle.

2. Always reserve the highest degree of influence for your own judgment, thoughts, and beliefs.

3. Look at the motives of those you allow to influence you.

4. Reflect on your own self-worth and self-esteem as it relates to the need for approval and support from influencers.

5. Look for honest influencers and not those that just validate your thoughts.

6. Carefully and cautiously, allow someone into your inner circle of influence.

Awareness-Your Patterns

"Once in motion, a pattern tends to stay in motion."

J. G. Gallimore

Patterns are those recurring events in our lives and in the business world that create similar, if not the same outcomes. Patterns are also one of the more difficult pieces of self-awareness for people and intricately connected to the Law of Attraction. The bottom line is that you will continue to attract exactly what your continued patterns dictate until they are identified and managed.

Business Patterns

The reoccurring patterns in our business life are the easiest to spot and recognize because they have metrics associated with them. Measurable elements like revenue, jobs created, time in business and customer satisfaction provide great insight into successful (and the opposite) business patterns. Another common business pattern is a 'feast or famine' cycle that happens within a great many industries. Examine closely these patterns of successful business operation and learn to replicate those key factors in all jobs and businesses. If it worked well and created the success you desired, do it again. And again. Team member turnover is also a good one to look at to see if the patterns you create are healthy or not.

Conversely, a pattern of failure in business or becoming bored with a job or function in a matter of a brief period can be telling. Even in times of success, the pattern that led to past failures should be examined. Why did the past business ventures fail? Why were you bored and jumped from industry to industry? Look for both points of satisfaction and dissatisfaction in job functions and look closely at why past entries into business failed. One that I have seen over the past 20 years is entrepreneurs that burn through partners and employees like some people change shirts. This is most certainly something to examine and reflect upon.

Personal Habit Patterns

Also, relatively easy to spot but much harder to manage or change are personal habit patterns that are often rooted deeply in behavior, belief, and emotion. In some cases, they also carry chemical dependency and social needs as well.

Successful patterns are those in which you *consistently* take care of yourself through exercise, diet, activity, learning, saving, investing, healing and growth. Meditating and jogging two days in a row does not a successful pattern make. Harmful patterns are those in which the continued behavior creates ill effects on health or even your financial position.

Other personal patterns to consider as you become more and more self-aware include trusting (overly skeptical or overly trusting), use of money, managing time, reactions to pressure situations, and if we choose to react in negative emotions (hate, revenge).

Relationship Patterns

Now the examination of our patterns begins to get tougher. All of us have had friends and acquaintances that share how their three failed marriages, six subsequent relationships and the kind of people they are attracting are all the fault of those other people. The truth is that we attract the people in our lives based on the patterns we live and our external projections. If you are attracting awesome, healthy people in your life and they stay connected to you for an extended period (sometimes forever), keep doing what you are doing and identify some of your great projections you are putting out there. Create a mirror of your behavior to attract the kind of relationships, both personal and professional; you want in your life.

Oppositely, if you are not attracting quality, long-term relationships (this even applies at work), look at what you are projecting and why the wrong people migrate to you. Some people are just a bug light for chaos, cheapened interactions, and short-term, toxic encounters. As my father told me, "you catch what you go fishing for".

Blame, Justification, and the River in Egypt

The evil demon that prevents the self-awareness of our patterns is the three-headed monster of blame, justification, and denial. Each of these block us from seeing how we create our own patterns and more importantly, how we can change them. Work on not attributing your patterns to others, explaining them away and denying that they exist. The painful truth is that we create our own patterns by action or inaction, and it is up to us to identify them and make changes when needed.

Changing Patterns

The great news is that no pattern in our lives or work is cemented in cosmic code and all of them can be changed. The first step is obviously to identify both the short-term and long-term patterns that serve us well and those that need to be changed. Note the good. All patterns have some good associated with them and some are all good stuff. By noting what is good, we can reproduce the quality outcomes and relationships we want to have in our lives.

Bad patterns are not changed in whole. They are only addressed in the behavioral (sometimes very small) pieces that create them. You cannot just change a bad pattern of broken marriages and relationships by saying so, you need to look at the individual behaviors that caused the dysfunction and tackle them individually and over time. I think my dad would call that 'changing bait'.

You will also want to track your changes and patterns (did someone mention journaling?) to see your results and provide yourself with the reinforcement needed to create new and great patterns in your life.

1. Identify your patterns related to business, personal life, and relationships.

2. Note and list which of those patterns are desired and serve your life well and which need to change.

3. Identify the specific behaviors that create both good and bad patterns.

4. Continue to repeat the good behaviors.

5. Work on reducing and ceasing the bad behaviors.

6. Journal and note your progress.

Awareness-Projections

"It's not what you look at that matters, it's what you see."

Henry David Thoreau

Projections are those things we put out into the world that allow others to judge us and, more importantly, dictate how they interact with us. They are a moderately complex set of behaviors that include body language, tone, physical appearance, and the words that come out our mouths. The importance of projections is that these are the most easily correctable piece of personal behavior and they have tremendous influence over how the world sees you and chooses to relate to you.

Your projections are your magnet for other people and situations. Simply put, you will receive from others what you choose to project. Unfortunately, personal projections are also a common blind spot among adults. Many people just do not know what they are projecting to others and what those signals are attracting.

The balance of this section will look at common projections and offer tips to tuning them without sacrificing the core of you.

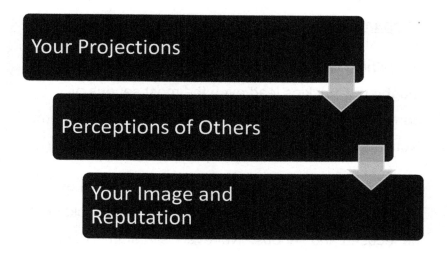

Super Serious Dude (Labeled without Gender Deference)

This was my wake-up call in the early 90's when a team member gave me the nickname of "Stomper" because of my tendency to walk fast and move with a sense of purpose through the office. What I was projecting was high urgency, high self-importance, and little regard for anything around me. This one is found in verbal and tone responses when interrupted and you always project a hurried approach or overly share about how busy you are or how important the work is that you are doing. A simple fix on this one is to lighten up and slow down. A gentle reminder that the world does not rotate around you and your project can also be useful.

Flippant Soul

Everything is a joke. Every response starts with laughter. Chuckles lead even the most serious of conversations. Smart ass comments are ever-present. Nothing is taken seriously.

Fun is great and everyone should have as much as possible but sometimes we need to arch our backs and be focused and serious. Not every situation is bubble-blowing giggle worthy. Learn when to be serious and when your comments and projection is too much for the situation.

Spiritually Smug

One projection set that is becoming more prevalent and common is spiritual smugness. It is certainly awesome that you found God (or more accurately that God found you) and you now have inner peace, detachment, and total enlightenment. Awesome. Now, stop judging the rest of us and sharing your path. Your path is yours, not ours and the constant pointing out of either your peace and happiness or our failure to find it will not serve you well in connecting with others.

Quiet, Aloof and Genius

One of a couple of unfair projections, quiet is often misjudged as aloof or even arrogant. Again, not fair but what you are projecting will determine what you receive back from others. You may be legitimately quiet and introverted, but the world sees it differently. The same with smart people (an affliction I have never had to deal with). They are unapproachable because of vocabulary or command of a subject in a very directive tone. Learn to be more open and outgoing when around people and keep some of your genius in the garage.

Flirt and Charm

The line between good manners, charm and being overly flirtatious is thin. This one too is unfair in most cases and there are different standards (unfairly so) for women and men. Much of this is wrapped in non-verbal signals such as walk, leaning in during conversations and in tone. The point of knowing this projection is to allow us to connect more solidly and genuinely with people and not based on projections we do not desire to have in our lives.

Bitter Pill

Everything is wrong, everything is bad, and the world is an ugly, ugly place. This projection, usually through a combination of verbal and tone signals is very distancing of others. No one wants to be around the person that sees nothing good in the world. Find the good in things, share it, and learn how to park your criticality.

Invisible Transparency

Transparent is great. It really is. It is awesome to be a genuine person, flaws, and all. However, there are those people that over disclose to the point that they have nothing left to share to anyone. They have told the whole story, names included, to anyone that will listen. We all have that over-disclosing friend and that is one we tend to avoid. Keep some boundaries on what you share with others to maintain respect and credibility.

You Are What You Wear

Not everyone wears Prada, but the harsh truth is that people judge us by our appearance and that judgment will affect connections and relationships with others. Wear booty shorts and see what you attract. This is not to say we must be dressed to the nines in all situations, but we should be aware that our outer appearance will indeed dictate many of the responses and reactions we receive from other people. And to be intellectually honest, we do it to others as well.

As a reminder, you will attract exactly what you project.

To get a great handle on your projections:

1. Find a trusted source of honest feedback to tell you about what you are projecting.

2. Look at positive connections and relationships you have and what kept them strong, lasting, and healthy. Those are projections to keep.

3. Look at relationships that were not healthy or long-lasting. What were the projections that brought those people to you?

4. Connect projections back to your patterns. Do you have a set of projections that create either positive or not healthy patterns in your life?

5. Projections are not a single element. Look closely at non-verbal signals, tone, and your words to really become self-aware of what you project to others.

Awareness – Your Emotions

"If you are tuned out of your own emotions, you will be poor at reading them in other people."

Daniel Goleman

This one is a big deal and one that is often overlooked by even the most self-aware people.

Your emotions drive your attitudes and beliefs. Your attitudes and beliefs drive your behavior. Quite simply, if you want to achieve lasting change, you must look deep into your emotional composition.

Emotions → Attitude and Beliefs → Behaviors

Emotions Include:	Attitudes Include:	Behaviors Include:
Joyful/Elated	Positive Expectation	Communication Tone
Happy	Belief in Positive Outcome	Praising/Thanking
Positive		Empowering
Neutral/Content	Belief something will be Better	Risk Taking
Overwhelmed	Hopeful Outlook	Facial Expressions
Hurt/Disappointed		Innovation
Angry		Relationships
Depressed		

Emotions are a powerful part of being human and we cannot ignore the impact that they have on our life and our success. We cannot run from our emotional composition.

Dr. Daniel Goleman, the father of emotional intelligence, found that 80% of our reactions, responses, decisions, and choices are driven by emotion. Many of us start with a logical and analytical approach but at the point of choice, we default to an emotional reaction. Although painfully simplistic, think about some of your eating choices recently. Many of those were driven by emotion and not by a logical choice.

Our emotions come in a range and two sets of ranges. Love is the super-emotional driver of all positive emotions. Fear is the driver of all negative emotions. Positive emotions range from satisfaction to joy while negative emotions can run the gambit from despair to boredom.

Do not fear or automatically reject negative emotions. All emotionally healthy people touch a full range of emotions frequently and negative emotions help us to know what we do not want in our lives and around us. The key with negative emotions is not to deny them, but rather to accept them and then move out of that state quickly and correctly. Do not avoid them or deny them, just deal with them rapidly.

Managing and working with our emotions is not about eliminating them. The psychological term for that is psychopath. The key to great emotional intelligence is to:

- Understand them

- Work to reduce the negative, fear-based emotions

- Live in a steadier state of positive, love driven emotions

Emotional Composition

100	• Joy
85	• Passion
70	• Enthusiasm
55	• Positive
40	• Optimism
25	• Hopeful
10	• Content
0	• Boredom

LOVE

ae•gis
LEARNING

Emotional Composition

0	• Boredom
-15	• Pessimism
-30	• Frustration
-45	• Overwhelm
-60	• Anger
-75	• Hate
-90	• Jealous
-100	• Despair

FEAR

ae•gis
LEARNING

Emotions and Physical Energy are Connected

Another easy visual. When you are in a higher emotional state (joyous, happy, satisfied), your physical energy is higher. You have the energy to execute your ideas and drive your passion. Conversely, when your emotional composition is lower (anger, frustration, grief), your physical energy is lacking.

This is an important barometer to keep in mind as we continue to look at your emotions. Listen to your body's energy.

Most Common Emotional Frame

Healthy humans have ups and downs in their daily emotional composition. There are times of joy, times of satisfaction, times of overwhelm and periods of dark. All part of a normal day on the planet. Not every moment is butterflies and mugging selfies as Facebook would have us believe.

However, within the fluidity of human emotion comes a common resting spot. It is a place where, over time, people's emotional composition comes to settle. This is the spot that both you and I seek to understand. This becomes the emotional baseline that can then be used for prescriptive actions to improve overall emotional health.

It's Not What You Think

When asked, most people will respond with a higher level of emotional composition than accurate at the time. This is due to a couple of factors including lack of emotional awareness and the desire to project a better state of emotional health to others and the outside world. In my experience, most people will respond to the query about emotional composition with where they would like to be instead of where they are actually at currently.

So, to get to your real emotional composition, some tracking is needed. My encouragement is to look at your most common emotional composition over 30 days. Also note your emotional high and low points for each day as well.

The Reconciliation to the Truth

As you track your own view of emotional composition, ask a friend, significant other or trusted team member to give you the same information daily. Ask her or him where they think you are at and note that as well.

As the above equation is true that emotions drive behaviors, your behaviors are a tattletale of your emotional composition. The feedback from a trusted source is based on your behavior they observe. Your tone, your body language, how you approach situations – even if you overcompensate with trying to be happy. You cannot escape what your behaviors tell others. Frustrated tone comes from a frustrated person.

After 30 days of your own observations and 30 days of feedback from a valued and trusted source, you can see your most common spot. I hope that with 30 days of self-examination you were also able to be more self-honest with your typical emotional state as well.

To deeply understand your emotional composition:

1. Track your emotional high and low points for 30 days.

2. Track your most common emotional settling points for 30 days.

3. Get feedback on your emotional composition and note it for 30 days.

4. Note your baseline state of emotional composition.

5. Listen to your body's physical energy signals in this process.

Other Points of Self-Awareness

"What I am looking for is not out there, it is in me."

Helen Keller

In this journey of deeper, more meaningful and affecting self-awareness, we have looked at many of the components of the real us. We have examined motives, influencers in our lives, patterns of behavior, projections, and emotional composition. To round out our view of self, there are just a few more to examine.

Your Identifiers

The labels you attach when someone asks what you do or who you are can be quite telling. Do you self-identify with work? Do you have to add a title to the answer? Take a close look at how you respond and what that might say about yourself and project to others. Some of the most common self-identifiers include the need to use title or the brand name of the workplace because they add artificial prestige. The healthier choice is to focus your identification on either life role or your purpose.

Your Judgments

Judgments are a complex set of thoughts that become labels for others and us. They can be as simple as a passing thought about a fellow driver's ability to navigate traffic or as complex as a near-medical diagnosis. Examining how we judge others gives us some great perspective on how we judge ourselves as well. Are we overly harsh or critical of our performance and life? Do we create false expectations for based on our internal judgments?

Authenticity

The buzzword of the 2016 through 2020 is authenticity. Unfortunately, many people use the label of authentic to be a fool. Authenticity is not about living outside the boundaries of society and human respect, as some people will use it for, but rather a congruence with personal core values and beliefs. Does being authentic give you permission to curse inappropriately, treat others poorly and be harsh when delivering feedback (think about telling your wife how a dress looks)? Of course, it should not. Being authentic means keeping your behavior consistent with your true beliefs and values. If you speak love, you should project love. If you profess forgiveness, then that is what your behaviors should reveal to others. Being authentic means being consistent and not running away from the filters and rules of a decent humanity.

Your Purpose

Discovering why you are here may be the final piece of great personal awareness. We are not built to just pay bills and plan our funeral. Understanding, and then connecting to, your greater purpose and calling will greatly drive your success.

Do not be too harsh on yourself if you have not yet discovered your calling and purpose. There is no time frame required and some people will find it in their 20's while others find it in their 80's.

Deep inside of you is a combination of your points of passion, what you are good at, and what the world values greatly. That is a great starting point to discover your purpose.

Please note, just because you are passionate about something does not make it your purpose. I am passionate about singing. I am horrible at it. No one values it. Not even the dog. Point of passion, or what stirs your soul, is a great starting point. However, you must also assess whether it is valued, and if you are any good at it, or if you are able to develop competence in a short period.

To find your purpose or begin the process:

1. Identify your points of passion.

2. Identify what your talents are.

3. Reconcile the commonalities between items 1 and 2.

4. Check to see if the world values your points of passion and what your talents are.

5. Test for economic viability.

6. Construct a plan to bridge from your current position and function into your purpose.

Conclusion

Not every piece of self-awareness is pleasant to examine. Sometimes it can be downright painful to reflect and know yourself on a deeper level. This deeper and authentic view of yourself can now lead to the significant and lasting changes that you desire. Quite simply, you cannot fix or move the dial until you know the starting point.

And now you have a much clearer understanding of the real you.

1. Look at the labels you use to describe yourself. Do you use titles or are you more connected to life role and purpose?

2. Examine how you judge yourself and other people. See how those judgments limit both yourself and how you connect with others.

3. Work hard to not be as self-critical, impatient, or limiting with yourself.

4. Become authentic by being consistently connected to your core values and beliefs. Act in congruence with those values.

Changing-The Tools to Unlock a Heart for Leadership

"We are what we repeatedly do. Success is not an action, but a habit."

Aristotle

Unlocking your heart for leadership and life success will require a set of tools to utilize and embrace those practices within that tool set. For our purpose here, a tool will become a habit or vessel for our practices. The practice will be layered over that set of tools.

As a best practice, it is highly encouraged that you use time and task management helpers until the tools become habitual and second nature for you. Quite simply, add a daily task to your list for each tool until it becomes automatic. The other best practice related to these tools is to become unrelenting and unyielding in doing them daily. Every day. Rain or shine. Feeling good or not.

A funny dichotomy I have witnessed over the last few years is how unyielding people become without their workout routine, and that's great, but when it comes to managing their emotional composition or heart, it becomes hit or miss. If you can solemnly ritualize a physical routine or diet, you can easily make heart and emotional power a part of your day as well.

Self-Care

"I have come to believe that caring for myself is not self-indulgent. Caring for myself is an act of survival."

Andre Lorde

An old saying about the light from an empty lamp must ring true for us here. We cannot lead, be successful or have any energy to serve the world if our fuel has run out. Most of us know that is related to rest, exercise and even diet but rarely do we apply that principle to our emotional composition and heart. When we are drained emotionally and spiritually, we have no chance to be a light to others (a big part of being a leader) and our ability to execute our ideas are dramatically reduced.

This is about taking care of you. The real and inner you with the same commitment that you use to take care of your external body. Be gentle with yourself and own the responsibility for self-care. It is no one's responsibility except yours.

Self-care is the ultimate empowerment. It is using a set of tools and creating some practices that allow you to be insulted and resilient from outside sources. Think of self-care as a super-vitamin for your heart and emotions. Another way to look at self-care is to compare it to your physical health practices. When you are healthy through exercise, diet, and the like, you are less likely to catch a cold and, if you do catch it, you can fight it off more easily. Emotional and heart-based self-care is the same. You may still have down moments and off days, but you will recover quickly and have them much less frequently. Empower yourself and create a meaningful protection for your emotional and heart power health with self-care.

The first stop in using self-care as a powerful tool is to back off the hyper-criticality of yourself. Leaders and successful people have a high propensity to be self-critical, to demand more of themselves and to expect perfection in all situations. That drive to be better is extremely healthy and useful but the criticality when you don't achieve those benchmarks is not. This can become a common self-defeating behavior as well, especially when not checked or not balanced. Self-analysis and debriefing when something did not happen the way you wanted it is healthy and good. Beating yourself up unmercifully and continuing to remember those failure points is not healthy on any level. Be gentler and forgiving with yourself.

We need to commit to a routine and habit of self-care that includes managing our heart and emotions on a regular basis. To commit, as in treating that with the same respect as we treat the management of our physical selves. Without this, we are a system that is not firing on all cylinders and we will never reach our full potential.

A couple of notes of warning about self-care:

1. Self-care can become self-absorbed and isolated very quickly if not properly balanced.

2. Self-care can, when not balanced with the needs of others, become an almost narcissistic pursuit of personal happiness.

3. When nothing else matters but personal happiness and health, relationships, and

connections to the rest of the world will be strained.

To avoid these pitfalls, look at your commitments to self-care, versus how much time and energy you apply to outward pursuits and purpose. Our purpose is not merely to be happy and whole, but rather to use our happiness to serve others and ultimately live out our purpose on this blue marble.

Two unbalanced examples to consider:

> The person who starts their day with 30 minutes of meditation, an hour of yoga, two hours at the gym and then followed by reading, a smoothie for lunch and an evening run.

The weighting in this example is incredibly internal and focused only on self-care. The external will suffer for this person.

> Another person is in constant giving and doing mode. Juggling three charitable functions, a more than full-time job, part-time budding business on the side, two children and a couple of hobbies. Friends and social interactions constantly. Never a piece of 'me' or down time.

This one too, will eventually collapse because of the total lack of self-care and complete focus on external service to others and being busy.

The answer then for effective self-care is to carve out some balance between care for self and the care you provide others. Not a perfect 50-50 split but something reasonable where you are able to meet your obligations to the world, take care of others around you and still have a committed course of action to taking care of your mind, heart and body. The litmus test is if one area (care of obligations, others, or self) is being neglected or suffering from lack of time, then more balance needs to be achieved. Listen for yourself to say phrases like "I wish I would have" or "I wish I could have". The statements of regret, both in personal life and work, are signs of needed balance between self-care and outward care.

Authenticity

"Authenticity is when you say and do the things you actually believe."

Simon Sinek

As buzzwords go, none have risen more to the top of the heap quicker than authenticity. It has become a catch all for over-sharing, exhibiting bizarre behavior and even just being a fool. When pressed about behavior, there are people who will respond flippantly with "I'm just being authentically me".

The authentic you is quite complex and some of it needs to be let out and some of it needs to remain very private to you and you alone. For our purposes moving forward, and to use authenticity as a useful tool in unlocking the heart, authenticity means a couple of things:

Being self-honest in who you are. Not the self-crafted narrative that is playing now but the true you that has great strengths and some challenges. A balanced and honest portrait of you.

Understanding who you want to be and how you want your life to play out. Connecting deeply with why you are here and ensuring you are always moving in the direction of purpose.

Aligning your core beliefs with your actions on a consistent basis. Not speaking of one thing and doing another but living your values and connecting the behaviors.

Becoming comfortable with dropping any masking or pretense and just being you, within the boundaries of societal rules and responsibilities. Great that the inner you is a nudist, however you are an attorney and that is frowned upon in court. There has some restraint to keep society running smoothly, not alienate others and remain as productive members of a community. More on this subject in the next couple of sections.

So again, as we move forward, authenticity will be an awareness of what we believe and project, it may not always be an accurate us and we need to align our real, authentic selves with our purpose and our hearts for ultimate success.

Be authentically you. Unless you're an ass, then be better.

Time Investment

"Someone is sitting in the shade today because someone planted a tree a long time ago."

Warren Buffett

Before you completely go nuts with the "I don't have any time" mantra that is far too common, let us look at perspective and where to find the time to unlock your heart.

Our investment of time starting out will be about five minutes. From there it will move to about 20 minutes and maybe top out at a half hour per day.

For some of you, this is going to be hard to find. Our lives have become so consumed with being busy and facing the demands and pressures from both work and home that an extra few minutes is a luxury saved for vacation.

Challenge yourself to look for the needed time to unlock your heart in some of your current rituals and habits such as:

1. Social Media-the time parasite of the millennium. What starts as a quick view of notifications or looking at a couple of friends can easily become hours of browsing relationship statuses and cat pictures.

2. Television-a common distraction and place where some time can be recovered.

3. Emails and Text Messages-not as urgent as you think. Age them a little and answer them in groups instead of being a reaction slave to the red bubble or golden envelope.

4. Web Surfing-quick browse and 20 YouTube videos later, an hour is gone.

These are just a couple of examples of where we can find the time to create a self-care and heart unlocking habit set. Each of us has different spots in which we can find some time without sacrificing the quality of our lives or jeopardizing important work tasks and projects. We are talking about just 20 minutes.

The time you select matters as well. The single best practice to block time for your heart and emotional composition practice is first thing in the morning. Your physical energy is high, the house is usually quiet and there is a certain peace with the morning. If you wait until later in the day, you may lack the energy needed and you will have dozens of built-in excuses for not doing it. Do it early and avoid any potential loss of time or commitment.

One other best practice related to the time for self-care is to do it after some physical activity or exercise. Many people wake up with their minds going 140 miles per hour with everything that needs to be done during the day and playing their calendar repeatedly in their heads. Exercise, even the tamest, walking-the-dog version, can provide some clearing of this before you begin your heart work.

Space and Place

"Change your location and you just might change yourself."

Eric Weiner

Just as the time commitment for heart and emotional care matters, so does our location. In fact, time and location go together to creating a successful leadership self-care practice.

Comfort matters. Pick a spot that is comfortable for you. Your chair, your couch, anywhere that is absolutely your spot. I have three. One inside, one in the garage and one outside on the patio. Based on weather, time of year and just adding some variety, I rotate through using all three.

A couple of other environmental things related to location:

1. Televisions, radios, and any other distractions need to be removed.

2. Lighting for your spot should either be soft and dim or lighted by the sun.

3. Telephones must be silenced and only used for timer purposes. Most phones have settings allowing only the alarm to play during silent mode.

Describe the boundaries of your time and location to your family and significant others. Again, this is not a big space or a large amount of time. After a couple of iterations, they will not even notice you are disconnected for a few minutes in 'your spot'.

From here on, this will be your spot and used for your beginning work on unlocking your heart.

Journaling

"Journal writing is a voyage to the interior."

Christina Baldwin

Time to go shopping.

Not for just anything. It is time to buy a journal.

The process of writing is a key element to learning and creating powerful new habit sets that will unleash your emotions and heart in a positive way. Simply put, writing behind thinking, doubles the learning and the chances of successful long-term outcomes.

What It Is and Isn't

First, you do not need to spend hundreds of dollars on a leather bound, custom etched journal. If you do, that is fine but certainly not necessary. Mine is an 89-cent spiral bound, wide ruled notebook from Walgreens. This version has a red cover. All that you need is a place for some thoughts and assignments through this journey.

One page per day, maybe two. A page here and there for some special notes.

This journal also becomes an incredibly valuable tool to look at where you have come from and the progress you have made in unlocking your heart. Several executives I coach send me their journal entries daily and the differences between day one, day ten, day forty and year two are amazing to see. You will see the same as well and be able to celebrate your growth in heart and emotional energy.

One other best practice to share is the use of technology versus the handwritten form of a journal. Making a running Word document, using an app, or creating a spreadsheet would certainly work for journaling but there is something missing and some elements get lost in the process. The best recommendation is to do a handwritten journal.

What's in It?

The contents of everyone's personal journal will be a bit different. The commonalities start with a notation of the day and time. Other common elements for journaling will include a brief description of where you are at emotionally, items of gratitude (much more on that later), meditation practice (more on that shortly) and even some things about physical health. During our process here, we will also add some intentions for the day and anything that needs to be cleared out of emotional baggage to move forward successfully and powerfully.

You will find, as I and many, many others have found, that once you get into a journaling habit, the words, format and what you want to commit to paper will come easily and flow from you. This journaling sweet spot is an awesome feeling and you will wonder why you never did it before.

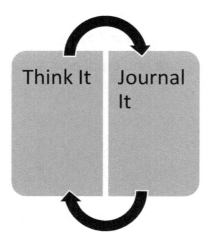

Think It   Journal It

To begin and engage in journaling we want to:

1. Acquire a journal or notebook.

2. Acquire a pen or pencil (yes, I'm being a smartass).

3. Write your name on the cover. Maybe add an ominous warning that this journal is private.

4. Note the date, day of the week and time at the top of page one.

5. Write a little note about how you are feeling physically and emotionally.

As this book progresses, steadily more and more will be added to your daily journaling routine. After that, the entries will be up to you and how you choose to continue to manage your heart and emotional composition.

Meditation Practice

"Meditation is not making your mind quiet. It's a way of entering into the quiet that is already there."

Deepak Chopra

Here's a brief list of people who meditate:

Michael Jordan

Bill Ford (Ford Motor Company)

Oprah Winfrey

Arianna Huffington

Madonna

Steve Jobs

Hugh Jackman

Rupert Murdoch

Clint Eastwood

Marc Benioff (Salesforce.com)

Nicole Kidman

Russell Simmons (Def Jam Records CEO)

In addition, another quick list for you. Publications that have endorsed and researched the value of daily meditation:

The Wall Street Journal

New York Times

Harvard Business Review

The Economist

Forbes

Fast Company

Inc.

Meditation is not a practice for a fringe set of people who self-isolate in the Tibetan Mountains or run off to

Honduran love fests. Meditation has become a mainstream practice of those who want success, peace of mind and to unlock their inner strength. This is part of the time investment described earlier and our results are going to be noted in the journaling practice.

There is no right and wrong to meditation and please - run from anyone who tells you otherwise. There is no required music, chanting or mercifully, spandex. You do not have to do anything but commit to the practice and try some recommended ways to get it going. After your initial first few weeks, you will be able to explore new and different techniques to help you achieve even more in meditation.

One important point about mediation and multitasking is that you cannot. For a good number of years now, I have heard from people who proclaim that they are meditating while running, biking, hiking, walking, watching TV, etc. Sorry but no, you are not. Meditation is a focused activity that requires a singularity – mindful if you will - approach. When you are running, biking and all the other activities, that becomes your primary focus and you are probably able to do some thought clearing and maybe even some positive replacement work, but -

you are not truly meditating. Do not shortchange the process by trying to add something else to the mix.

Also, note that early on, we are going to be distraction free. No music. No phone app. Nothing but you. There is certainly a place for music and guided meditations but that is not quite yet.

Mindfulness and meditation are not synonyms. Mindfulness is a set of techniques and practices designed to provide presence, relief from stress and enhance focus. It can be engaged on a moment's notice and will be discussed further a bit later. Meditation is a purposeful daily practice that will help you achieve mindfulness and much more.

Brief History of Meditation

The first appearance of documented meditation occurred around 1500 BC in ancient Hindu scripts. The 5th century had the earliest documentation of Taoist and Buddhist meditation practices. Judaism, Eastern Christianity, and Western Christianity have developed meditation practices ranging from the 10th to the 14th centuries.

In the 1960's, meditation regained western culture popularity with the introduction of various forms of the practice in North America. It was during this time that meditation had a close association with various forms of yoga.

Fast forward to now and meditation is a mainstream practice encouraged by workplaces, practiced in halls of religious worship, and endorsed by the successful as a primary tool in their development and growth.

Meditation is not a new thing. It is a very validated and scientifically and historically supported thing.

Meditation 101-Getting Started

"When you arise in the morning, think about what a precious privilege it is to be alive; to breathe, to think, to enjoy, to love."

Marcus Aurelius

Our starting practice is going to look a lot different than what it will be like after a month or so, but we are going to begin small and ease into a more robust version. Trying to jump in too deeply, too quickly, may contribute to many people stopping meditation and giving up on it.

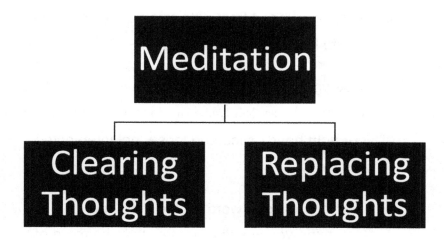

Go to your spot first thing in the morning or after some physical activity or exercise. Although meditation can be done at any time, the morning will be the most powerful for you and have the highest probability of not being interrupted and being quiet.

1. Sit comfortably in your chosen spot or location.

2. Stretch your right arm high above your head and hold it there for a few seconds. Repeat with your left arm. Now stretch with both arms together above your head and hold them up there for a few seconds. These stretches should be pulling your back straight and loosening up your shoulders and arms.

3. Rotate your head from side-to-side and front-to-back to loosen your neck up a bit.

4. Place your hands in your lap or on your legs. Put the palm of your left hand over the knuckles of your right hand. Nice and loose, not intersected or tense.

5. Think of one good word for the morning. Something you would really like to have more of in your life - like love, peace, joy, or happiness. This will be the word and thought that is locked in during this brief meditation.

6. Take a deep breath in through your nose; hold it for a few seconds and think of the word you chose during the inhale. Exhale through your mouth with a purposeful push. Repeat this process three times with each subsequent inhaled breath being a little deeper.

7. Now relax and for the next minute concentrate solely on your breath but in a normal cadence and pacing. While inhaling normally through your nose - think of your power and intention word - and exhale normally from your nose.

8. Repeat the arm stretching exercise above to close out your first meditation practice.

Congratulations! You have just meditated. The total time invested is probably somewhere around three to five minutes. For the next week, continue this practice and gradually raise your time of focused breathing to three minutes.

Meditation 201-
Intermediate Meditating

"You have the answer. Just get quiet enough to hear it."

Pat Obuchowski

The intermediary practices of meditation are not much different than what was described previously. To continue to grow the benefits of meditative practice, you will want to add:

1. Sitting cross-legged with your back as straight as comfortable for you.

2. Place your hands in palms up position on your thighs or near your knees.

3. Lightly connect your index finger and thumb on each hand. Adding this touch point provides some neuron-stimulation that aids focus and meditation.

Allow your breath to flow naturally and begin to add the practice work described later in the book. Expand the time to five to seven minutes.

The time allotted to the tool of meditation is probably up to about ten minutes now. A ten-minute investment that will pay tremendous dividends daily and long-term in unlocking the power of your heart.

Graduate Level Meditation

"Only in my deep meditation do I come to know who I really am."

Sri Chinmoy

From here, the growth in your meditation practice is on you. There are a great many resources available to you to add some music, set intentions, control thoughts and still your mind but the tool is now in your hands. There is no right and there is no wrong in meditation. The only failure is if you do not continue to try and grow. Create this tool to your needs and your unique heart needs. Let it evolve. Let it grow organically. Avoid anyone who tells you how to do it 'correctly or that you must adopt a branded yogic style. It is about you and not them. Make meditation part of you.

In the journey section of this book, you will discover more things to add to your meditation and more practice elements to achieve. However, please, do not rush this and be flexible and gentle with yourself on the days it does not seem to flow quite right.

Feedback Partner / Truth Teller

"Feedback is the breakfast of champions."

Knowing and trusting yourself is awesome.

Getting the truth about yourself from someone else is priceless.

To have someone in your life that will provide you honest and straightforward feedback is an incredibly powerful tool. Truth telling includes both the great headway you are about to make, and the difficult pieces that you do not see in yourself. This person is the go-to when you need input about your projections, what others see in you and some balance in how you view your emotional composition. This person is also the cheerleader-in-chief that comments when you are becoming different, happier, and more successfully in tapping into the positive energy of your heart and emotional composition.

The real trick here is to find that person. My best recommendation is to avoid craigslist ads and random encounters at the grocery store. The other, and serious, recommendation is to not use your spouse or significant other. That one strikes people as odd because it is that relationship that is most intimate and, in many cases, the most loving and caring. Unfortunately, it is for those same reasons that the spouse or life partner is not a useful source for your feedback. A spouse or significant other loves you unconditionally and wants nothing but the best for you. Some of the feedback you need to move forward in unlocking your heart is tough and not a vase of roses.

More Advanced Tools and Practices

"Motivation gets you going but discipline keeps you growing."

John Maxwell

Now that your toolbox and set of practices is becoming more robust, we can move on into the set of practices that truly unlock your heart and remove the obstacles from your growth and actualization. Compare this to now engaging a set of blueprints for our project where previously we were working only from a site plan. We have the saw, hammer and nails and the next sections are those step-by-step (not IKEA-like) instructions and design. The end of it all will be a work of art that is you and your unlocked heart and emotional power. It really will be glorious.

The following practices are presented in purposeful order. The first few will provide immediate jump-starting of your heart and clear some mud away from your emotional composition quite quickly. The remaining practices have significant impact as well but must only be done after the first few practices are engaged. These practices can be categorized in three ways:

Clearers

Those practices that eliminate past hurts, disappointments, baggage, and other blockages. Mud cleaners if you will.

Energizers

Those practices that add love-based emotional energy to your heart. They are the ones that replace what was cleared out and cleaned by the Clearers.

Hybrids

Not going to give much away on this set of practices but suffice to say there are those that both clean and energize. Sounds a bit like a nutritional supplement advertisement but there are those practices that both release the mud and add the power of positive emotional energy.

Finally, at the end of the book, and please do not skip to it, is a timeline that discusses the integration of the tools and practices over a 40-day period. This outline is a quick view guidance to creating the best you possible with full heart integration with your skills and other great attributes.

The Amazing Power of Gratitude

"Gratitude is not only the greatest of virtues but the parent of all others."

Cicero

For a leader or any person, the practice of gratitude provides:

1. Ability to see the good in others and situations

2. Clearing of darkness, bitterness, disappointment, hurt and anxiety from the heart

3. Openness to increased positive outcomes

4. Attraction of more positive events in which to be thankful

The consistent practice of gratitude is one of the most powerful tools available to leaders and anyone. It is also very predictive of success in both work and life. When gratitude becomes a way of life, it will open your heart, clear out a lot of bad junk and provide the room for many more blessings to come to you. Gratitude is a starting point to unlocking your heart for better leadership and a better life.

What is Gratitude

Gratitude is the expression of appreciation, both internally generated and externally communicated. It is a feeling of thankfulness and true joy in something you have or someone in your life.

The power of gratitude rests in the internal feeling generated by being thankful. This piece is all about you. It feels good to remember our blessings. This takes some of the mud off our hearts.

As if that were not enough, the power (some say superpower) of gratitude becomes when it is shared with others. This is where multiplying; compounding and diametric expansion of the power comes into play. Now, instead of just you feeling better - you have affected, in an incredibly positive way, someone else. They now have a choice of continuing the expansion by being appreciative of others or even reciprocating your gratitude. Over time and consistency, gratitude will change the emotional composition and create a wave of positive belief for individuals, companies, and communities.

And wait, there is still more (no, there will not be a sales offer for Ginsu knives coming). Gratitude has the unique power of re-framing a dark, difficult situation into bearable and, even positive. Think for a moment about one of the most challenging things you have faced in the past few months. Now look deeply for some positive qualities in that situation. Did you learn from it? Were there some great qualities in that difficult person that are now covered in the mud of anger? Were you able to overcome the obstacles and continue with life? Did you move forward, despite the lingering pain and hurt? If you can answer yes to any of those, you can be grateful for that difficulty. And when you do, it feels great.

Where Should I Look for Gratitude?

Sadly, many people reserve their appreciation for something big. A raise, promotion, winning the lottery, delivery of a big project all rises to the level of easily common gratitude.

Genuine gratitude and the power that comes with it is found in the usual and the often-overlooked pieces of everyday life. Successful gratitude practice will focus on thankfulness for the necessities, the challenges and all the resources we have been provided. And without any 'but' statements connected to them.

Beyond the ordinary, another measure of a successful gratitude practice is to remain thankful and appreciative when times are difficult and challenging. Almost all people can be grateful when things are going well but what about when circumstances are hard. This requires a resolute and self-disciplined approach to look for the good, see the lessons and appreciate the challenges for what they are - small obstacles in the road of life.

A final measure of a gratitude practice is if you can be genuinely thankful and appreciative for someone else and a blessing they have received. Even if, perhaps, it was a something that you wanted. Can you be thankful, grateful and celebrate a coworker's promotion when you also wanted that job? Can you express gratitude for the happiness of someone's interpersonal relationship when you wanted that same relationship? Particularly challenging scenarios and when you can answer yes to the above, your gratitude practice is on very solid ground.

The greatest gauge of how you are doing will be how you feel. If you feel a warmth in your heart, a satisfaction when expressing gratitude and even note a smile creeping in on your face more often, your gratitude practice is progressing very well. Also look at your own compassion, as it is the cumulative effect of gratitude. Grateful people are more openly compassionate to others.

A leader should be thankful every day for:

1. Family and Friends

2. Her or His Team

3. The Employer or Company

4. The Challenges Solved or Lessons from Them

5. Resources Available to Lead

6. Critics and Naysayers

7. The Life Necessities of Food, Water, Shelter, Clothing and Transportation

Saying Thanks is Not the Same as Gratitude Practice

When introducing gratitude as a restorer of leadership heart and emotional composition, the consistent rebuff is "I always say thank you" or "I am always grateful". And they are probably right but that is not the practice of gratitude and it does not have the lasting impact and power of creating an intentional and mindful practice.

To truly unlock this great heart power, begin the practice of appreciation and gratitude by:

1. Taking 30-60 seconds to clear your mind of clutter and the bouncing thoughts that affect many of us.

2. Use two to three minutes to think of things in which you are thankful or grateful. Nothing else but those thoughts for that time.

3. Note five to ten items in which you are thankful or grateful in daily entry journal form. Be sure to date the entry.

4. Of the five to ten gratitude notations, make sure at least one and preferably two are directly about something you did. That's right, thankful for you

and your own actions. Give yourself a little appreciation and thankfulness here.

5. Also ensure that at least one of the grateful notations is about a challenge, struggle, loss, hurt or pain. Look deeply for the good in something that was difficult at the time but brought a positive outcome or great lessons for you.

6. Pick one of the items of gratitude and purposefully express it to the person involved. Tell them. Send them an unexpected note of appreciation. Do something for them. It doesn't really matter how you do this but express it sincerely and from the heart.

7. And the last step is to use the shampoo method on this practice: wash, rinse, and repeat. Consistency is key to the power of gratitude. Everyday. Even on vacation.

Freedom through Forgiveness

"The weak can never forgive. Forgiveness is the attribute of the strong."

Mahatma Gandhi

Forgiveness provides us:

1. Peace from past conflicts, issues, and challenges

2. Closing resolution with people and situations

3. Space in our emotions and heart for positive thoughts and feelings

4. Freedom from the burden of past hurt

5. Capacity to allow people to grow and overcome their transgressions against you

6. Ability to create relationships in the current state and not bogged down by the past

7. Enhanced personal resilience

With gratitude, forgiveness is one of the biggest cures to restoring the heart to a point of love and your attitude to a consistent positive state. The mud-freeing that occurs when forgiveness is practiced for the first time and then consistently thereafter is nothing short of amazing.

What is Forgiveness

Often forgiveness is misunderstood and associated with forgetting. You hear things like "just let it go" or "forget about it" and that is a common misconception. We humans do not have an erase button or delete key to remove a memory. The memory stays. Forgiveness gives us the power in how the memory is framed and the capacity to create positive overwrites of the prior memory.

Forgiveness is also not some grand spectacle where the person who wronged you is involved. Real forgiveness is quiet and there is really no need to share with the person being forgiven. Many times, the person who wronged you forgot about the event long ago or doesn't even have an ounce of awareness about it. This is all about you and not about anyone else.

For our purposes, forgiveness will be the solemn promise and vow that the event or person we are forgiving will not influence any future interaction or event. So, by forgiving someone, I am not promising to forget it happened. I am promising that whatever the past event, I will not allow it to change how I deal with that person moving forward.

In a simple analogy, say someone cuts you off on the freeway during a long commute. Forgive them quickly and you return to safe and alert driving very quickly. Failure to forgive that other motorist and your attention is focused on harsh judgment of him or her, your anger and perhaps even revenge. Here, failure to forgive distracts from the ability to drive safely and could have dire consequences.

Accountability and Forgiveness

In a working environment, the most common objection to the practice of forgiveness comes from the apparent exclusivity of accountability and forgiveness. As a leader or person of success mindset, accountability is a core principle. Team members must be accountable for their performance and behavior. Vendors must be accountable for their promises of delivery. Partners must be accountable for the terms of the agreements they executed to work with you.

And all of that is true. Accountability is a foundation of success and leadership and must not be compromised.

Far too often in a business environment, accountability becomes a lifetime proposition. If someone commits a transgression, makes a mistake, or has some significant challenges, then sadly, that becomes their career-long legacy. In my work as an executive coach and with other teams of leaders, the phenomenon of someone being on a radar screen for a past transgression is extremely common as is the failure to provide any pathway off that radar screen. Yes, that person made a terrible mistake three years ago and you held them accountable for it. Now is the time to stop defining them and judging them on that mistake and allowing them the chance to recover and giving yourself the freedom from this baggage as well.

Accountability should be swift and fair. Behind that, forgiveness should be equally swift.

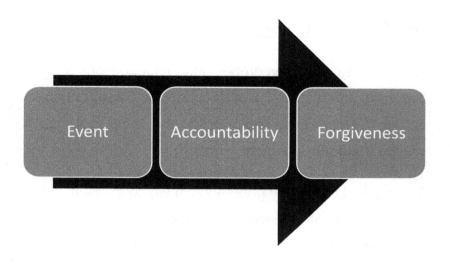

The equation of workplace and leadership forgiveness will look like this:

1. Judge and assess an event, performance, or behavior.

2. Use defined accountability tools such as corrective feedback, documented discipline, or even termination of relationship.

3. Grant forgiveness and not have the event affect any future interactions with that team member or other person.

Who and What to Forgive

Showing my age, I remember Schoolhouse Rock on Saturday mornings. A noun is a people, place, or thing. Similarly, forgiveness eligibility has the same dynamic. It can be a person, event, or yourself.

The easiest to identify population in which to grant forgiveness is other people. If someone does you wrong, then they become eligible for forgiveness. This becomes the straightforward process of connecting a hurt to the person inflicting hurt. Anger because you had to correct mistakes of another team member is simple to connect to that team member. Upset because your spouse barked at you can be pinned directly on him or her. Anyone that you attribute wrong or hurt should be considered for forgiveness.

Events should also be forgiven. These are those times and situations in our lives in which things went wrong. We learned the lessons, hopefully not repeating any of them, and now is the time to forgive and move forward in full heart and emotional health. Examples of event forgiveness includes blocks of work and career time, stretches of personal relationships and even single choices made by you or others. Stop talking regret and grant freeing forgiveness.

The hardest forgiveness to grant will be to you. That's right. Forgiving yourself for your mistakes, poor choices, and events in which you were responsible. Many people can grant real forgiveness to others easily but hold deep frustrations, regrets, disappointments and worse about themselves. Yes, you caused something bad. You paid the price. Now is time to forgive yourself and get this ugly, caked mud off your heart.

First Time Clearing

The first clearing of past wrongs, including your own, will be the most difficult. Some of these people and event have been living on your heart and influencing your actions for years or even decades. This first event will not be easy, and it will not be quick. Depending on the depth of hurt and wrong, you may have to go back and forgive a couple of times to truly have it cleared.

As a practice, use this process the first time around:

1. Note three to five people or situations that you need to forgive in your journal.

2. Leave the list alone for a couple of days.

3. Include thoughts of who has wronged you, what baggage you are carrying around, and any situations, which still bring you pain or angst, in your daily meditation. Let the thoughts flow freely to you in this setting.

4. Examine the list a second time and add another three to five people or situations that need clearing forgiveness. Ensure that at least two and hopefully more of these are forgiveness of self.

5. Leave the list alone for another couple of days.

6. Take a final look at the list and ensure you have most of who and what needs to be forgiven, including those things you need to grant yourself forgiveness.

7. Next to each item, list a date certain in which you will forgive that person or event or you and release the negativity associated with it. The first date should be within the next day and it should also be the simplest or easiest situation to forgive. The person that cut you off in traffic and caused a minor irritation should be at the top of the list

compared to complex life situations and people that have wronged you greatly. If you are not yet prepared to set a date for all items on your list, that is okay too. Some dates can be out there for a bit of time to allow yourself the reconciliation and readiness to let it go.

8. On the date listed, add the words of forgiveness to your daily meditation. In the simplest form, it would sound like "Today I forgive XXXXX and promise to never let this event influence me" or "Today I forgive XXXXX and promise this event will never influence me again".

9. Congratulate yourself on this step. Be pleased with yourself. This is a big thing.

10. After your meditation, say your chosen words of forgiveness aloud and cross it off your forgiveness list. Continue until the list is gone.

The Forgiveness Practice

Beyond the initial clearing described above, events and wrongs happen regularly and need to be forgiven. The quicker you can make the event/person-forgiveness cycle, the healthier your heart and emotional intelligence. With this junk cleared regularly and daily, the room for great emotions, attitude and energy is almost limitless.

During the quiet and clearing portion of your meditation, search for those people or situations that may be weighing on you. Repeat the action steps above and forgive quickly.

As this process becomes a habit, you will be able to grant forgiveness on the fly and make it a natural part of daily self-care.

Giving

"We make a living by what we get, but we make a life by what we give."

Winston Churchill

The power of giving is tremendous and the value rests in not only what we provide but in what that giving, if done correctly, does for us. Giving is one of, if not the most, powerful clearing practices available to us. It will open your heart and emotional composition in extraordinarily strong ways.

First, giving is not just about money. In fact, some of the most meaningful giving will be related to donating your time and assistance to others. Money is needed by many causes but for the best heart unlocking impact, we are going to focus more on giving of our time, energy, and talent. There is a role that money will play in this but that will be later.

A giving heart is truly a joyous heart and a giving heart is one free from the baggage of negative emotions.

Give to Give

"Give freely to the world these gifts of love and compassion. Do not concern yourself with how much you receive in return, just know in your heart it will be returned."

Steve Maraboli

When we create an expectation of return, even for the simple craving of a 'thank you', we are creating a contractual business transaction and not giving. No matter what we give or how much, there can be no expectation of gain, return or even karmic credit given to us. True heart unlocking giving is crafted only when we are not concerned about the publicity, appreciation, or ultimate return to us but rather we are focused only on the act of giving and the recipient. Once you make the choice to give, if money, effort, or time, you cannot have any expectation of a return.

This is hard because many of us (me included) have bought into the need for common courtesy and at least an expression of gratitude from the recipient of our gifts. We brew quite a pot of indignation when that does not occur. Many others of us (again, me included) have created belief sets about the power of karma where if you do good for others, that good will be returned to you. There is probably some truth to that but receiving a positive karmic outcome cannot be a motivation to real giving.

Giving must be done from a position where you see a need, provide a gift of time, effort or money and there is no expectation created after you give.

Give without Condition

"Kindness is loving people more than they deserve."

Joseph Jourbet

Conditional giving is related to creating expectations discussed above but rather than a return, the giver puts strings on the giving. "Use this money to buy food", "I would give you more but the salaries you pay are outrageous" and "I will help you move but only if you don't invite (fill in name of undesired helper)" are some common types of example.

Similar to creating an expectation for a return, this conditional attachment to giving also destroys the personal value of giving because the darkness in our hearts is not released and probably grows. Giving must be done without any strings or conditions attached to have the desired value on emotional composition. When the money leaves your hand or donated time is committed, it must be up to the receiver in how it is used.

Giving at Work

"The smallest act of kindness is worth more than the grandest intention."

Oscar Wilde

Although changing, the workplace is not commonly associated with the practice of giving. This is unfortunate because that is where we spend the most time and often, have deep relationships that would benefit from the giving.

Workplace giving will be most often challenged by the perception of lack of time. This is a self-produced perception because your time can be spent on what you choose to prioritize, and you can always find some give-and-take to create giving opportunities. If you fight this dynamic, take a close look at your priorities and the legacy you want in the workplace.

Some great opportunities for giving at work include:

Mentoring Someone

The committed one-on-one relationship between a mentor and mentee is highly rewarding and valuable. Share your knowledge, successes, failures and build someone to reach their potential. A true transcendent experience.

Encourage the Discouraged

You know when someone is down or really struggling at work. Contribute a few minutes, encourage them, and offer support. Build them up and help them see their own light and good.

Participate and Engage

Organizations of all types and sizes are always looking for people to participate and contribute time on committees and enrichment efforts. Don't sit on the sidelines any longer. Volunteer, step-up and participate with your most valuable asset, your time, and your talents.

Create a Giving Campaign

Another opportunity to give at work is to really get outside your comfort zone and organize a giving campaign in your own department or division. When there is no organization-wide momentum or focus, create your own. Get some input from other and your team and then lead the way in giving. Run a coat drive, collect dry food or volunteer at the soup kitchen as a group.

<u>**Getting Close**</u>

"Never worry about numbers. Help one person at a time, and always start with the person nearest you."

Mother Teresa

One of the reasons that writing a check to a major charity does not provide emotional benefit and heart unlocking power is the degrees of separation from the beneficiary. Write a check to a mission fund at church and it goes to that church's office and treasurer, then to a national body, then to a group running the mission and then finally to end user. Lots and lots of separation and truly little connectivity, especially the emotional kind, to the receiver.

The closer you can get to the receiver the greater the impact on your heart. When you can distribute food, and talk to the homeless, the connection with the recipient is direct and strong. Much better than donating your coat is handing your coat to someone who is cold.

Closeness can also occur when your time is extremely valuable. Those of us that value our time more than any other resource will find great heart opening value when we give the time, we do not believe we have available. The adage of giving something to a busy person is pertinent here because great value is felt when you did not think you had the time to contribute or give.

You may also want to consider your relationships here as well. There is a high likelihood that someone close to you is in need. They may need some assistance, a little money or just a person to listen to them. This is a great opportunity to get close to the giving and make a big impact in someone near and dear to you.

Contributing Cold Hard Cash

"Generosity is giving more than you can, and pride is taking less than you need."

Khalil Gibran

Most people are generous. They give when they can and give when everything is paid, and they have extra.

When it comes to giving money and the unlocking power of the heart, unfortunately, this is not enough. In relation to money, to donate and have emotional changing value, the giving must come before personal needs and - in some cases - when you really do not have the money to give. This is an area to challenge your own personal comfort and even make some sacrifices for the good of others.

Consider these approaches to giving money and affecting your heart and emotional composition and energy:

1. Provide monetary contributions before any other bills or necessities are paid.

2. Sacrifice some personal comfort or luxury items to provide some money to give. Forgo a meal out or a trip and give that money to someone or a cause in need.

3. Give some money to a cause, charity, or another person when you do not know how it will be replaced or how you will cover the rest of your bills.

4. Schedule and budget your monetary giving like you would with any other obligation.

5. This is a huge paradigm shift for most people but with that big of a shift will also come a great sense of gratitude, clearing, and humility.

Laugh, Play and Have Fun

"Just play. Have fun. Enjoy the game."

Michael Jordan

The power of laughter, fun and play being curative for the heart and soul is well documented. A dear friend told me recently that laughter is good for the soul and she was right. The anecdotal evidence is equally as powerful. When you are laughing, having fun, and just generally enjoying yourself, your emotional and physical energy is higher.

Enjoyment also has a tremendous ability to unlock the desire to have more fun and an amazing side effect is that it will attract people to you like nothing else. People love to be around the smiling and fun and can't wait to get away from the grim and downtrodden.

Before we engage more fun, let's track back and see what happened to it. Because we all started with it and it was encouraged and promoted early on but sadly, we lost it. As children, our parents cooed when we laughed. People even tickled us to evoke that laughter. Everyone loves a giggly baby (the internet is full of them) and that behavior is rewarded and replicated.

As we begin school, play and laughter is programmed into our day. We have play breaks and physical education classes that are designed to produce active fun. Yes, not all memories of PE are great but generally, there was a lot of smiles and play.

Then adulthood crept in and we have been told to 'settle down', 'be quiet', 'stop grinning' and then of course, 'act professionally'. Somehow being an adult and productive member of society was equated to being joyless and losing our sense of fun and desire to play.

Fast forward to now and we see adults that struggle to identify what they enjoy or the last time they had a frolicking belly laugh. Play is no longer programmed, and we find it only as we have time. Perhaps worse yet, we participate in hyper-competitive or super-physical activities labeled as fun but really lacking any joy beyond survival.

Let's Find Some Fun

"Creativity is intelligence having fun."

Albert Einstein

To really unlock the power of fun, we must acknowledge that our society and workplaces are not very conducive to unbridled fun and the demands on our time and energy are tight so we must make fun programmed again. Just like grade school.

Adding the practice of fun to your heart and emotional composition power will require:

1. Create a list of things you really enjoy doing. Nothing you must do or feel accomplished about but that you just really like.

2. Create a list of those things that make you laugh and smile. This can include people, media (movies, television episodes, YouTube videos), books, cartoons, and the like.

3. Identify, and journal, the last time you experienced laugh-out-loud joy and the last time you experienced unrestricted fun.

4. Now add a time block of something fun and laugh provoking per day. Give yourself permission to take a laugh break. One of the best spots for this is at mid-day during lunch. Have a cartoon or funny video queued up and give yourself the joy of laughter to keep your day rolling along nicely.

5. Schedule a fun activity each week. Again, nothing that should be done but a block of time devoted to pure enjoyment. This could be an adventure, travel, reading, a movie, a comedy club trip or just anything, that is for your joyful pleasure.

6. Note in your journal both the change in your emotional composition and change in your facial expression.

Fun at Work

"Do not take life too seriously. You will never get out of it alive."

Elbert Hubbard

As with other things, human social needs most notably, people create the artificial boundary that fun has no place at work. Unfortunately, the qualitative evidence from extremely successful people and organizations speak otherwise. Fun at work is a great ingredient to keep your heart open and create a winning culture that drives results.

This certainly does not mean that work becomes one big party but what it does mean is that successful and heart-healthy people find a way to create a little fun during the day. Some ways to consider that include:

1. Build little fun breaks into your day where you privately watch a funny video (corgi puppies are awesome clowns, but I digress).

2. Encourage laughter in others through your own laughter and sense of fun. This will create a

perpetuation of the fun concept when others share it with you.

3. Lighten up! Except for a few people, no one has their hand on the nuclear button. Do serious work but do not take yourself too seriously.

4. Share some funny pictures (appropriate, G-rated, and with no political, religious, or sexual overtones) with team members and get them to do the same.

Fun Jump-Starters

"Work hard, have fun and make history."

Jeff Bezos

One of the most difficult challenges to beginning a practice of fun is the starting point. Here is a small, not conclusive, list of some activities that will bring a smile and warm a heart quickly to the idea of fun:

1. Skip. Yes, skip.

2. Whistle a tune.

3. Go to a variety store (Target, Walmart). Test a Hula Hoop. Publicly and with no apologies.

4. Hop. Not a full jump. Just a little hop or two.

5. Randomly snap your fingers for a few seconds.

6. Try a tongue twister or read a limerick.

Somewhere in this list you found your smile again. Maybe you even chuckled aloud. That is awesome and congratulations. The power of fun is within you (it always has been) and now is the time to let more of it out to help your heart heal and grow.

Removing Judgment and Blame

"Be curious, not judgmental."

Walt Whitman

Judging others and ourselves harshly is one of the most damaging heart and emotional behaviors that we humans engage in. The release of negative judgments will have a significant and lasting impact on emotional composition and overall heart-driven power. Judgment also closes our mind to possibilities and limits how we see others and the world. This one is a major game changer.

Unfortunately, it is also one of the most difficult to cure and keep in check.

The starting point must be one of acknowledgment and definition. Judgments are those thoughts about others in which a comparison to a way we would look or do something and is based on our values and beliefs. So if I drive ten miles over the speed limit in the left lane (and

I do), and I approach a vehicle cruising at speed limit, my tendency will be to judge that driver harshly based on my values and thoughts. The same goes for appearance, religious values, work ethic, and family composition and on and on.

For a more serious look at judgment, think of your spiritual values and how vested you are in those thoughts. Now think about how you view people of quite different values and how you choose to view them. Do you think of them as unsaved, infidels, unclean, ignorant, or even worse? This is certainly a dark scenario but not horribly uncommon.

The bottom line with judgment is that we do it. We do it a lot. In almost every encounter, we have, we create a judgment. Because those judgments are overwhelmingly negative in nature, they create a drag on our emotional composition, even if momentarily. The more we judge others poorly, the deeper and longer the toll that will be taken on our heart and emotional energy. The less we judge others and the quicker we can recover from a judging moment, the greater likelihood of sustaining awesome heart-based energy and emotional state.

And now for a realistic view of judgments. Based on our research for this book and the coaching we do around this subject, it does not look like this can be fully ever cured or subordinated. I have had the great luxury of being around and near some very enlightened and well-put together people that still have negative judgments. They may not always acknowledge it, but they do. This appears to be a hardwired part of either our neuron composition or such an ingrained behavioral element that it may not be fully erased. And this tendency to judge may never be completely understood.

For our purposes moving forward, our objectives related to being negatively judgmental is to reduce the amount it occurs and to recover quickly from the impacts of those judgments.

Origins of Judgment

Cognitive Biases	History with Someone	Expectations

The Marriage of Blame and Judgment

"When you blame others, you give up your power to change."

Robert Anthony

Blame is a toxic projection of judgment. When we assign responsibility for a fault or a wrong, we are acting upon the judgment that someone else is the cause of something that has affected us in a negative way. Judging others paves the way for blame and blame becomes toxic when it prevents healthy self-awareness and self-understanding and creates a lack of personal accountability for actions.

To wit: I'm late for my appointment because of the slow driver in the fast lane. My judging of that driver led to my blaming him or her for my failure event. The truth, and personal accountability, is that with better planning and leaving earlier, I would have been to my appointment perfectly on time.

Another example would be my boss has it in for me or doesn't like me. That is the blame for my career not moving along like I would like it to. The accountability is his not mine and that blame comes directly from my judgment of her or him as not a good leader or nice person. The reality is probably much more closely related to my performance, lack of relationship with the boss or even my own jealousy.

The ability to create a harsh judgment and assign blame is significantly easier than to own our choices, decisions, and mistakes. That level of personal accountability is difficult especially when the ease of judgment and blame rests directly in front of us.

Now this does not mean you have to take accountability for the totality of every event around you. However, it does mean that you must own your participation in it and a percentage of every event around you. You are neither a victim nor the responsible party fully for any negative event. Look at the tragedy of a natural disaster for a moment. You did not trigger the hurricane, but you did choose to live in a flood zone in a known hurricane area. You do not own the entirety of the disaster, but you must own the choice to live there, not affix blame and not be a victim.

As an emotion, helpless victim mode is an extremely low emotional position and some professionals will label it with clinical terms. Helpless starts with being a victim and avoiding accountability for our actions and decisions. That blaming begins with judgments of wrong about another person, group, or entity.

When being overly judgmental turns into blaming and victimhood, the urgency of managing our judgments becomes extreme.

Self-Judgment

"Discontent, blaming, complaining, self-pity cannot serve as a foundation for a good future, no matter how much effort you make."

Eckhart Tolle

As much as we cannot blame others, judge them harshly or skirt the responsibility of our own actions, choices, and decisions, you can also not judge yourself harshly either. This behavior of turning the very harsh judgment lens directly back on ourselves can be extremely self-defeating and drop the power of our emotional composition and heart.

Healthy, happy, and highly productive and successful people accept responsibility openly but look at the failure events only as a lesson and not something to be regretted or dwelled upon. The practice of forgiveness of self comes into play as you must own the failure, not judge others or yourself harshly, grant yourself forgiveness and move on quickly. Fail, own, and learn.

The criticality of self must be balanced with a view of your positive characteristics and strengths. Far too often people will remain focused on failure events and create a very harsh self-judgment of lack of value, worth or worthiness.

Equally, we cannot create a view of self-perfection either. Some self-help gurus and guides will lead you to believe that everything you do is without fault and all your actions are perfect. You, indeed, are perfect but your actions sometime are not. Healthy self-judgment will keep you positive while accepting your challenges without just shrugging your shoulders and sauntering through your life of perfection. You make mistakes. Own them, learn from them, and move on without being overly critical of yourself.

Reducing Judgment, Blame and Self-Sabotage

We sense and feel thoughts forming and those thoughts are going to translate into behavior and a change of our emotional composition and energy. To acknowledge and understand this is the beginning of reducing judgment, blame and self-sabotaging thoughts. We know the thought is forming. We can feel it and sense it clearly.

From this point, we can begin to reduce judgment of others by:

Creating a Pause

The pause between a thought and action can be extremely powerful here. When you acknowledge the thought or judgment, stop for just a mere second or two and allow your empathy and additional steps to kick in.

Genuine Human Empathy

The real kind of empathy is beyond saying "I'm sorry" or "I understand how you feel". It is truly putting yourself in the emotional or situational position of another person. This takes practice and work. Have you felt how they felt? Do you know someone of a similar condition? Those are the types of questions to spur and grow your empathy to reduce judgment. For me, the driver in the fast lane that evoked my anger looked a great deal like my dad and I remember how he struggled in city traffic.

Cease the Comparisons

Comparisons to others, their accomplishments, and the things they have accumulated and even their relationships are the fuel for toxic judgments. Stop comparing yourself to anyone or anything. You are unique. They are unique. All the situations are unique and inherently, comparisons become unfair. When tempted to compare to someone else, compare and compete only with the you of yesterday.

Acceptance

Adding an emotionally and mentally driven thread of overall acceptance is a powerful tool in reducing and removing judgment of others (and self). Acknowledge (this is the mental/cognitive part) and then accepting (this is the emotional driver) that people are different from you, have different values, and live different lives. It is neither right nor wrong but just different and that makes them and their actions okay. Battle your ego in self-defeating belief that your way, beliefs, traditions, and values are right. They are right to you but not viewed that way by others. As you would want others to accept you as you are, do the same for them.

Mantra

A mantra is a little saying that you keep in reserve that helps you re-direct your thoughts. This can be incredibly powerful when you know a harsh judgment is being formed. One of the best replacement mantas is "Be kind". Not complicated and extremely easy to remember, this should be thought and even quietly and privately spoken to help reduce our temptations to judge others.

Consistent and Persistent

Judgments of others are so pervasive that a consistent approach to managing them is needed to reduce these negative thoughts. Keep at it! Don't give up and do make some notes in your journal about your judgments and how the reduction process is proceeding.

The steps to reducing the blame on others is like removing judgment and equally requires a dedicated approach. Those steps include:

Pronoun Replacement

As you, driven by your thoughts, are about to blame, replace the pronoun (he, she, they, et al.) with the first-person pronoun of I and recreate the sentence. So instead of they did this, the sentence begins with I did this. The rethinking here becomes to put your part of the situation or event first. Own your part before establishing any fault or blame with others.

Pre-Forgive

Prior to casting blame on others, practice some proactive forgiveness. Yes, you stole my super-sweet parking spot at Target, but I forgive you. No need to wait for anger or frustration to build to create forgiveness. Grant it as a precursor to knowing those emotions will boil up.

Let the Past Be the Past

As judgment usually occurs in the present state (now), blame is usually cast in a past event. There is immediacy with judgment while there is past tense with blame. Judgment is about something occurring while blame is about something that has occurred.

With this step, we must consciously acknowledge an event happened (someone did us wrong) and there is nothing, absolutely nothing, we can do to change it. It happened, and it must now be released, with lessons learned, and without the toxicity of blame.

Deeper Analysis

When events are so strong that your initial reaction can be nothing but blame, some focused thought time will be needed to get passed it. Spend some of your meditation time after your blaming to see where you, your actions, and your choices own part of the event. Create a point in which you can say "it needed to happen" and then create an acceptance of your role in the event or circumstances. This may take a while for you to get there based on the severity of what occurred.

The final set of processes will deal with a propensity for being overly judgmental of ourselves. We are not going to pretend that we are perfect or create some illusion that all of our actions fit within some universal law, but we will craft a way to balance a healthy self-view without being overly harsh.

Recognize the Self-Doubt

Clearly acknowledge when your thoughts (and that nasty demon voice of negativity) begin to creep in. Make this recognition quick and don't let it gain traction in your head and emotional composition.

Encourage Not Criticize

Replacing – and doing so quickly - the self-destructive voice with encouragement is critical. Turning "I'm a failure" into "yes I can" or "I'm getting past this" must occur within seconds of first detecting the negative voice.

Remember the Successes

Take some time and go back to remember your successes and positive moments. Look fondly at pictures, stories, and recognitions that you have received. Remind yourself of the good.

Practice Self-Forgiveness

The hardest forgiveness you will grant is to yourself. However, it is extremely necessary when the voice of sabotage, doubt and negativity creep into your thoughts and heart. Yes, you made a mistake or a poor choice, but it is past, and it is time to forgive and move forward.

Perspective

What may seem devastating and life altering in the moment, really is not. Tomorrow, the sun will rise, you did not impact the rotation of the earth on its axis and you get a new chance to succeed and be happy in this very moment. Perspective is about accepting the consequence of your actions and then recognizing that more time and opportunity exists. In some cases that is an opportunity to correct and in other cases it is an opportunity to move on in good emotional health.

Leadership Judgment Conundrum

"Good judgment comes from experience, and a lot of that comes from bad judgment."

Will Rogers

A challenge for leaders is to correctly execute a significant part of their functions and fiduciary responsibility to their organization is to use great judgment without becoming hardened by being judgmental. In a simpler form, great leaders need to judge the performance of others, assess business situations, and make choices, sometimes-hard ones, based on that judgment. That is a big part of being a leader. Evaluating team member performance is judgment. Looking at the competition is judgment. Reviewing key metrics and data require judgment.

So, the juggle for leaders to exercise great judgment without becoming judgmental is built around where this process occurs. If the judgment is cognitive, analytical and without emotional bias, it is appropriate. This objective view of team members, processes and other business needs is what the organization expects from you.

When the judgment comes from clouds of fear-based emotion including jealousy, resentment, anger, or frustration, then you are being irrationally judgmental. This has no positive value to a leader or any person. Here is another case in which you know and sense when your judgment is rooted in objective logic or if it is being driven by negative emotions.

Intention Setting and Attraction

"Our intention creates our reality."

Wayne Dyer

Creating an intention is a great practice to move heart power and emotional composition and to build lasting strength with it throughout a day. Intention setting is using a word or short phrase to define your purpose for this day and longer. It creates a baseline target or objective as well as a powerful reminder for you.

Intentions must be phrased in the form of a positive and not the removal of a negative. An intention of "stop smoking" will not work while "live healthy" just might. Similarly, an intention mantra of "be nice" will create a pattern of niceness while "don't judge" or "don't be rude" will simply reinforce the presence and use of the negative state. Look for the desired outcome and not what will be eliminated.

The most frequently discussed intention set is the contrast between scarcity and abundance. This is the gospel of abundance that many gurus (used without deference to religious affiliation, they come in all denominations) preach. Simply, an intention of abundance is the desire to create wealth and have material things. When used to recognize the abundance we already have or to be more open to the possibility of abundance in our lives, it is a powerful intention. When used as a Christmas wish list, it will most certainly not work.

Scarcity is the opposite of abundance and is a dangerous intentional mindset because it locks someone into always scratching for basic needs. To the extent that a changed intention to abundance opens possibilities for more than simply basic needs, it is powerful.

From the perspective of heart and emotional composition, setting intentions provides a regular reminder and focus point that keeps us from falling deeply into any negative state. Another way to think about this is the intention mantra provides to the rally point when things get tough or challenging throughout any given day.

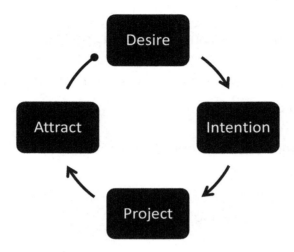

Another common intention is "I'm worthy". This intention set has multiple facets that include assistance with self-worth, reduction of guilt and the creation of openness for success that some people may consider out of reach.

Some common intentions include:

1. Be Strong (needing courage)

2. Open to Love (seeking relationship)

3. See the Good (help with gratitude and praise)

4. Be Kind

5. Live Healthy

6. Abundance

7. Peace (removing chaos and conflict)

8. Joy (increase in happiness, spreading happiness to others)

9. Here and Now (increased or return to mindfulness)

10. Calm (reducing anxiety)

11. I'm Worthy (self-worth or openness)

Not Voodoo

"When you have clarity of intention, the universe conspires with you to make it happen."

Fabienne Fredrickson

There is nothing mystical, cult-like, or opening the gates of hell about intention setting or creating and using a mantra. This matter of simple neuroscience and psychology clearly tells us that we are and will be what we tell ourselves. Our internal voice is incredibly powerful and when set to an intention of positive outcomes, our emotional composition and heart will follow.

By contrast, when our internal voice is dark, pessimistic, negative, and downright gloomy, our emotional composition and heart power have no chance of recovery. Mastering our emotional power requires keeping our reinforcing voice and thoughts consistently positive.

Intention setting is also at the core of the Law of Attraction. As mentioned previously, you will attract what you project, and you will project what you consciously process or manifest. Intention setting allows us the opportunity to create a powerful projection that will attract what we want in our lives.

The use of intention also gives us a great way to visualize a better tomorrow, a better way, and a better life. Visualizing the better creates a path for us to follow and the knowledge that better truly exists for us and that the better is within our reach and control.

Creating and using intentions require:

Desired Outcome

Select a desired outcome or objective for the next month and beyond. Good intention setting is more than just for a day and takes a long-term view. Spend time on this about what you really want to show up in your life and don't pick something arbitrarily because it may sound nice.

Lock-In

Use your meditation tool to lock in the intention mantra during opening and closing breathing. Visualize what this outcome looks like and feels like. When meditated upon, this word or short phrase should be on the top of your mind and influence your thoughts during the day.

Make Reminders

The complexity of life and work will come calling quickly and setting some simple reminders of the set intention will assist us greatly. Set a phone alarm reminder, post a couple of notes, or send yourself a repeating note. All those work great.

Share Your Intention

An incredibly powerful tool to assist your intention setting is to share your intention or mantra with a feedback partner or other trusted person. Tell them what you are doing and why. Ask them for feedback over the next month. This level of coaching-type support is priceless.

Mindfulness

"You can't stop the waves, but you can learn to surf."

Jon Kabat-Zinn

The easiest way to think of mindfulness is to equate to the present moment. At its core, mindfulness is about being present and at peace with the present situation. The key requirement is to still the mind and the emotional drivers that get our minds spinning, and to keep our focus clearly with what is currently occurring.

Unlike Intel Dual Core Processors, which can accomplish many things at once with equal skill, we reduce our effectiveness dramatically when we are all over the place. The sometimes charming 'butterfly' phenomenon of easy distraction and trying to observe in more than one place will ultimately fail. Our mind, as driven by our emotional composition, can do one thing well and moving onto the next. Mindfulness assists us in using this power to its fullest potential and keeping us clearly in the present moment.

The Value

"It is never too late to turn on the light."

Sharon Salzberg

The benefits of the practice of mindfulness are well documented and robust. One of the earliest signs that your mindfulness is taking root will be that your listening improves. And not just by a little but by a lot. Do not underestimate this value as it is often one of the most glaring missing success factors in people.

Another huge value of mindfulness becomes the reduction of the effects of stress. When you are mindful and in the present state, there is no anxiety about the future and no regret for the past. The only thing that matters is the now and removing regret and anxiety add excellent value to reducing your reaction to stress. The past is done, and the future will take care of itself.

The reported benefit of increased focus also has immense value when mindfulness is practiced. Your focus will drive your results and keep you moving towards key objectives, purpose, and mission. Clinically, the practice of mindfulness has been shown to reduce the impact of ADHD and ADD in trials and studies.

When combined with the practice of gratitude another piece of amazing evolution takes place. Your concern about other people's feelings increases and your tendency to just blurt something out (sometimes done in the name of being authentic, authentically being an ass) without regard for the emotions of others is reduced if not eliminated. The focus and presence of mindfulness with the heart awakening of gratitude produces this magnificent outcome.

Practical Mindfulness

"The present moment is the only time in which we have dominion."

Thich Nhat Hanh

The real value of mindfulness is the ability to summon it at any time and in any situation. Unlike yoga or meditation (quickly visualize whipping out a yoga mat during a meeting), mindfulness can be practiced on the fly and under any circumstances. With your heightened self-awareness, you know when your focus is waning, pressure is building, and you are generally not in the present moment. When you first sense this occurring, engage your reminder (discussed below) and bring yourself back to the present moment and the needs at hand. You can also take a clearing breath to help you focus and eliminate some of the guilt and regret from the past or anxiety of the future. Using a reminder word or mantra like 'calm' can also help refocus into the now.

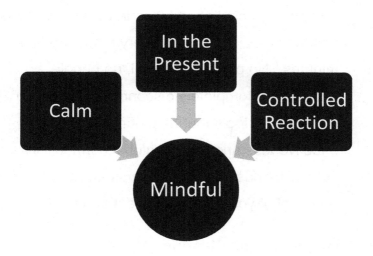

To generate mindfulness, begin to work on the following:

Quiet and Still

The first step in becoming more mindful is simply to find yourself a time to be. Just be. In perfect physical, mental and emotional stillness. Not for hours or days but starting with just a few minutes without noise, distraction, or interruption.

Detach

This one will challenge many people to the core of their being. Detach from everything for a few minutes. No phone, no email, no people, no television. Completely disconnected as you try to be still. The tools that help our efficiency and effectiveness and give us global connectivity are not our friends for these few minutes. Turn your phone off if you can or silence it at a minimum.

Breathing and Clearing

With inhale and exhale breaths, focus only on your breathing. Allow this process to clear out the thoughts, anxiety, and tension you are currently carrying. Just breathe and think of nothing else but your breathing. When another thought tries to pop in and take over, acknowledge it, and send it away by re-focusing back on your breaths. This will take a little practice and time but over a week or so it will become much easier to clear out the clutter of your mind and create a still spot for yourself.

Some people try to listen to music during this process, but our recommended best practice is to not do so until you have developed the practice more fully. Music can be distracting, become the focus rather than just clear, and still.

Use a Queue

Also, well documented is the use of a queue to help you get back to mindfulness quickly. Many people have used earlobe tugs to remind themselves to calm or to focus. The most effective practice we encourage is a finger and thumb connection (mudra from Hindu and Buddhism). This simple act is especially effective when using mindfulness in a practical application during the day. When mindfulness is needed simply grasp your thumb and index finger (or middle or ring or any) together and hold it together with light pressure on both hands. This is your new reminder to become mindful.

Awareness

After you have cleared and created a place of distraction-free stillness, start to observe your surroundings using all your senses at one time. What are the smells, sounds and sights that you observe? What is happening around you? Where are you and what is happening? Even in perfect stillness, there are things occurring. A dog moving about, a bird chirping outside, wind whistling are all examples of things to become aware of and observe. This focused awareness practice will assist you in producing practical mindfulness throughout the day.

Being Visionary and Being Present in the Moment

Leadership requires vision for the future. It is a competency that needs to be mastered for leaders at all levels in an organization.

So how can you be mindful, in the present moment, and still be visionary and look to the future?

Easy. A visionary and mindful leader will create the time and space to think about the future and better ways of doing things in a programmed and mindful manner. Not in the usual clutter of a day or week at the office but rather by setting aside time to plan, review strategic objectives and create a vision for the future. This should become a regular part of a leader's routine. Become a mindful visionary.

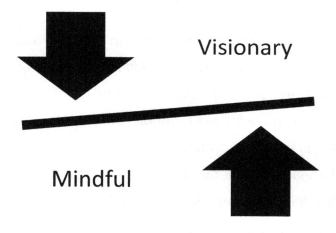

Grieve, Cry and Move On

"How lucky I am to have something that makes saying goodbye so hard."

Winnie the Pooh aka A. A. Milne

Unresolved and un-grieved events in our lives take a huge toll on our emotional composition. Until fully grieved, they remain in the background pulling our hearts to overwhelm, guilt, anger, and regret. Even with all the work done in gratitude, forgiveness, fun, mindfulness, and intention; an un-grieved loss will keep us from unlocking the full potential of our heart and emotional power.

When my dad died, I immediately launched into super-strong, logistics managing, support for everyone else mode. And did it marvelously. Unfortunately, I failed to grieve his passing until many years later. Similarly, with the loss of my mom, marriage, and company; I never processed the grief and it took a horrible and compounding toll.

Many of you have unresolved grief events as well and some will scoff at the use of the words grief or grieving when talking about job loss, job change, relocations and moves, loss of a valued co-worker, or the failure of a venture. Death of a loved one is not all that requires grieving.

The act of grieving is one of clearing and cleaning. It does not remove the memory of a loved one or valued event, but it does reconcile that past and puts us clearly back into the optimistic and hopeful present. Unresolved grief events will always have, even if just subtly, a dragging impact on our heart power.

Take Care of Your Physical Self

"Your body isn't a temple, it's a home that you'll live in forever. Take care of it."

Colin Wright

Lord knows that I am not a role model for healthy living. The things that I eat and sporadic exercise I get would give anyone pause.

The connection between your emotional, mental, and physical health is undeniable. When you feel good physically, your attitude, demeanor, and emotional composition are better. The converse is also true. Do you remember how surly you were the last time you had a head cold?

As you work on your mental and emotional well-being, this is a perfect time to start watching what you eat, getting more regular exercise, and paying attention to the signals that your body provides. Look for some opportunities to workout, walk, become more active, and slow down the intake of junk food.

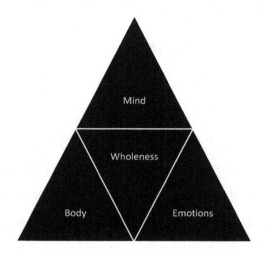

The Journey and Plan

"The rich invest in time; the poor invest in money."

Warren Buffett

This section is a daily guide to jump start the unlocking of your heart and releasing the power of your emotional composition. It is a day-by-day outline of the best practices and the pieces that were previously narrated. Now you get to combine the learning and place it into powerful action.

Journey Summary

Days 1 – 3	Preparation
Days 4 – 8	Meditation
Days 9 – 12	Gratitude
Days 13 – 17	Forgiveness
Day 18	Check-In

Day 1

Go Shopping

Outcomes and Practices

1. Purchase your journal.

2. Label it as yours.

3. At the top of the first page, write the date and time.

4. The only entry for today is to write "The Beginning".

Day 2

Your Space and Time

Outcomes and Practices

1. Select the time of day that you will commit to for your daily self-care.

2. Block this time on your time management tools and calendar.

3. Select a spot for your daily self-care work. Make sure it is comfortable and as free from distraction as possible.

4. Tell your family or other stakeholders about your intention for self-care, location, and time. Ask them respect and support this.

5. Note all the above in your journal for today's entry with the date and time at the top.

Day 3

Feedback Partner

Outcomes and Practices

1. Spend your first five minutes of self-care thinking about whom you could ask to be your feedback partner.

2. Document your choice or couple of choices in your journal for today's entry. Be sure to include the date and time at the top.

3. Sometime throughout the day, talk to your chosen feedback partner and tell them you will be relying on them for some honest feedback.

Days 4 - 8

Meditation

Outcomes and Practices

1. Perform the starting stretches described in the meditation section of this book.

2. Spend a few moments and think of a positive intention word for the day.

3. Breathe in through your nose, hold that breath and blow it out through your mouth.

4. Repeat for three iterations, each time holding the breath a bit longer. During the inhale, think of your intention word and play it out in your mind.

5. Continue breathing at a normal cadence with inhale and exhale through the nose. On each inhale, the intention word needs to be present in your mind. Concentrate on the breathing and intention word.

6. Journal, with the day at the top of the page, the approximate duration of each meditation and your intention word for that day. Consistent use of an intention word is helpful (i.e. use the same word for a week or two).

7. Begin tracking and noting in your journal your most prevalent emotional composition using the guidance scale and your high and low points.

8. Ask your feedback partner for some feedback about what you project to others.

Days 9 - 12

Gratitude

Outcomes and Practices

1. Continue the meditation practice (including stretching and intention word) from earlier.

2. Add a little time to the meditation to clear your mind completely. No words of intention. No purposeful thought patterns. Let your mind free and allow anything to come in. Be still and let your mind talk to you a bit.

3. Continue tracking your emotional composition including most common spot, highs, and lows. Add some feedback on someone close to you and how they see your most common emotional composition point.

4. Process and think about the feedback you received about your projections. How can you change behaviors to modify how others see you?

5. Identify your influencers using the circle method described earlier.

6. Note in your journal five things that you are thankful for today. Make sure that one of those are about an event or action in which you participated, or you had a significant influence (be thankful for something you have done).

7. Spend a few moments after meditation reflecting on those items. Think only in terms of gratitude and appreciation.

8. Express your appreciation and gratitude to someone noted on the list.

Days 13 - 17

Forgiveness

Outcomes and Practices

1. Continue the meditation practice (including stretching, intention word and mind clearing) from earlier.

2. Continue tracking your emotional composition including your most common spot, highs, and lows. Add some feedback on someone close to you and how they see your most common emotional composition point.

3. Continue the gratitude practice and journaling of the same.

4. Think about some of the patterns in your life and at work. Note them in your journal and describe the patterns you want to continue and those you want to end.

5. On a separate journal page titled forgiveness, list 3 or so people or events that you need to forgive.

6. After two days, return to the forgiveness list and add more entries.

7. After two more days, return to the forgiveness list and add any final entries. Next to each entry, list a date certain for when you will release and forgive the person or event. Make sure the list has some items of personal forgiveness (forgive yourself) included.

Day 18

Check-In

Outcomes and Practices

1. Continue the meditation practice (including stretching, intention word and mind clearing) from earlier.

2. Think about how you are doing now compared to how you were doing 17 days ago. In free form, journal your thoughts and experiences during the past 17 days. Put your pen to the paper and let your thoughts and feelings flow freely.

Days 19 - 23

Giving

Outcomes and Practices

1. Continue the meditation practice (including stretching, intention word and mind clearing) from earlier.

2. Continue tracking your emotional composition including your most common spot, highs, and lows. Add some feedback on someone close to you and how they see your most common emotional composition point.

3. Continue the gratitude practice and journaling of the same.

4. Check your forgiveness list and see if there is anything you need to add, complete, or extend.

5. Think about some decisions and choices you made and how your motivations and motives drove those choices.

6. Look for opportunities at work to provide assistance or mentor a team member.

7. Look for opportunities in your community to offer your time and talents to worthwhile causes.

8. Review your practices of financial generosity to make sure no strings are attached, and no expectation is created.

9. Your journaling should be easily filling a page by now and maybe even moving into two pages or more.

Days 24 - 28

Laughter, Fun, Play

Outcomes and Practices

1. Continue the meditation practice (including stretching, intention word and mind clearing) from earlier.

2. Continue tracking your emotional composition including your most common spot, highs, and lows. Add some feedback on someone close to you and how they see your most common emotional composition point.

3. Continue the gratitude practice and journaling of the same.

4. Check your forgiveness list and see if there is anything you need to add, complete, or extend.

5. Get some help from your feedback partner about what changes he or she has seen in you and the progress you have made. Continue to seek this feedback and work on behavioral blind spots.

6. Identify the activity that provides you the most fun and joy and think back to the last time you were able to do it.

7. Think about times when you laughed, really laughed, not some controlled chuckle but a full-on belly laugh.

8. Schedule a fun, play or laugh-inducing activity weekly. Be sure to let your family know and make sure it is something that you love and not a compromise activity.

Days 29 - 33

Grieve, Cry, Move On

Outcomes and Practices

1. Continue the meditation practice (including stretching, intention word and mind clearing) from earlier.

2. Continue tracking your emotional composition including your most common spot, highs, and lows. Add some feedback on someone close to you and how they see your most common emotional composition point.

3. Continue the gratitude practice and journaling of the same.

4. Check your forgiveness list and see if there is anything you need to add, complete, or extend.

5. Continue your fun and play ritual.

6. Think deeply about any loss or changes that you did not provide yourself with ample grieving time and space.

7. Note in your journal those events in which additional grieving and clearance are needed. You may want to look at this list a couple of times to see if it is complete.

8. Select a date that you will grieve and let go of the hurt associated with those events.

9. Commit solemnly to letting go of that hurt forever. Remember the event or loss but release the pain and suffering.

Days 34 - 38

Judgment and Blame

Outcomes and Practices

1. Continue the meditation practice (including stretching, intention word and mind clearing) from earlier.

2. Continue the gratitude practice and journaling of the same.

3. Check your forgiveness list and see if there is anything you need to add, complete, or extend.

4. Continue your fun and play ritual.

5. Review your emotional composition tracking for the last month. Look for trends related to events and people that produce changes in your emotional composition. Also look for general upward trends in your average emotional state. This is a huge positive indicator for you.

6. Check in on and think about your physical energy during the last month. Are you seeing a positive trend there?

7. Think about interactions that you had over the last day or so. How did your judgments about the person or situation change or limit the interaction? How many times did you create a judgment based on history or appearance? How many judgments were not complimentary or slighting rather than generous and open? How many of your judgments of others had no basis in fact or how many created or were based on jealousy?

8. Review and think about the times you placed blame, not true accountability, on others. Even if those weren't verbalized, did the blame affect your energy and emotional health?

Day 39

Check-In, Mindfulness

Outcomes and Practices

1. Continue the meditation practice (including stretching, intention word and mind clearing) from earlier.

2. Think about how you are doing now compared to how you were doing 30 days ago. In free form, journal your thoughts and experiences during the past 30 days. Put your pen to the paper and let your thoughts and feelings flow freely.

3. Think about how your practices of gratitude, meditation, forgiveness and giving can be incorporated into both your everyday work and life at home. Note opportunities to use these practices more regularly.

Day 40

Celebrate

Outcomes and Practices

You did it! Great job. You made it through a 30-day healing, recovery and unlocking journey. No small task and you should be proud of yourself and what you accomplished. This is a great achievement and you must feel good about it.

Not everyone experiences the same thing along this journey. Some, actually most people, will have a quantum leap in their energy, emotional composition and overall demeanor. People will compliment the new you and you will be hearing some great feedback.

Some people experience smaller, more incremental changes, and some people will encounter some setbacks as they progress through. Some will even get a little stuck on a step or stage of this process. And all of that is simply perfect. There is no right or wrong approach.

Now you need to celebrate where you are and what you have accomplished. Take yourself out to dinner. Buy yourself a treat. Tell people about what you have done. Whatever you do, celebrate your accomplishment. Bravo.

Day 41 and Beyond

Continuation, New Ideas

Outcomes and Practices

The first 40 days was just a start to your journey but from here, what it looks like is up to you.

My highest encouragement is to continue the meditation, journaling, gratitude, and forgiveness and giving practices. The rest will be your own creation.

Some things for you to consider moving forward include:

1. Research and add some music to your meditation.

2. Read about personal energy centers and chakras.

3. Consider a yoga class or two. Try out a couple of different styles.

4. Incorporate some reading and learning time into your self-care.

5. Look at personal reminder tokens or icons that will help you remember some key elements of your practice. Items such as a bracelet, pocket stone, or key chain can be nice reminders when things become challenging.

6. If you haven't already, add some physical activity prior to meditation to help your body and clear your mind.

Some Final
Encouragement

*"Just don't give up trying to do
what you really want to do.
Where there is love and
inspiration, I don't think you can
go wrong."*

Ella Fitzgerald

Nothing about this process is particularly easy and chances are you will experience challenges and obstacles along the way.

That's normal, okay, and to be expected.

The importance is not about the challenge but how you choose to respond to it. Stay the course and complete the journey, no matter how slow and no matter how disjointed.

One key point of encouragement is about your meditation practice. There will be days that you just can't summon a clear mind. Days you can't focus on your breathing. Days that you have so much going on in your head that you just can't clear and focus. And then there will be distractions. The totally expected and unpredictable mix of life that happens. The dog barks uncontrollably, the kids are up early, trash day. All normal and all okay. Just continue.

Recently, I was so hungry during a meditation attempt that all I could visualize is the Frosted Flakes in my pantry. Meditation lasted about 45 seconds and the cereal was consumed. I'm not particularly proud of this but I also realize that it is part of the journey.

Be gentle on yourself. Encourage yourself. Surround yourself with others that do the same. Continue on.

My Story

"Transparency breeds legitimacy."

John Maxwell

The path and guidance in this book also saved me from some very dark spots but that is not the point of sharing a bit of my personal journey here. My journey is a story of tremendous gain. A story of return. A story of completion. A story of reconnecting with purpose. A story of love.

During the past couple of years and more specifically since February 2017, I gained:

Lynn. The most beautiful girl in the world with whom I intend to spend the rest of my living days.

Improved relationships with my boys and understanding of them on a deeper level.

Connection and re-connection with genuine friends. Some dating back to high school, some I had not heard from in years.

True and meaningful appreciation for what I have and those people closest to me.

Exorcism and removal of the daily reminder that my needs, approach, vision, and path were wrong.

New friends coming from unlikely places and with depth of genuine connection.

New and returning team members connected by the thread of common purpose and vision. Not enough can ever be said about our first few people who chose to chase the vision and dream of making organizations and lives better.

Deeper appreciation for customers who wanted me and did not care about a company name.

A fresh start and newly founded company that returned to our core values and roots of helping people and organizations.

Passion and voice for my purpose returned in a big way. Muted for two or more years, being able to work on what is important, articulate what is

... true and good and returning to my core self was hugely important. Optimism and hope for the future, focus, calmness, and physical energy grew tremendously.

Return to a trueness, genuineness, and authenticity of how I operate daily and what I want to provide the world.

A passionate re-connection to serving others and helping make the world a better place.

To only acknowledge the gain would be disingenuous because the losses were large, hurt deeply but they also created the space for all the gains and deep appreciation. The losses include:

My wife of 30 years.

The 25-year-old company I founded and brought to a state of thriving. Stolen is the word my attorney uses.

My business partner.

Team members I hired, mentored, and supported.

A house, months of salary, any payment for the company, my credit, phone, and some other miscellaneous stuff that is now long forgotten.

Again, my focus is not on the loss but the recovery from loss and more importantly the path to that recovery. And it wasn't just a path to get "right", it brought great prosperity, peace, and abundance. My little two-year journey also included an emotional and mental collapse, complete with a stay in the hospital and a suicide attempt. Interesting side note that only one team member at the time, chose to visit me during my hospital stay and she joined us again.

The starting point in my return is the same as this book, deep self-discovery. I was able to find out quickly where roots of my unhappiness and untapped emotional composition rested. I discovered some un-grieved hurt from the loss of my dad, mom, and marriage. Faced some darkness in my heart and lived to tell about it.

If all of this sounds cavalier and brave, it isn't. I had a lot of help along the way and people by my side for every step. One of my biggest discoveries was that some people that I trusted the most and with everything were not deserving of that trust and only interested in their narcissistic and ill-gotten gains.

The great part about all of this is my story is it is not unique. The people that I and members of my team have coached through this journey have experienced the same and many times, even more dramatic results by unlocking the power of their heart.

About the Author

Tim Schneider is the founder, president, and lead facilitator for **Aegis Learning**. His mission, in total alignment with **Aegis Learning** is "Dedicated to Your Success". Tim brings passion, heart, and 25 years of successful experience to all leadership development projects, customer service initiatives and while building high performance teams. Tim is one of the most sought-after and in-demand speakers, training facilitators and individual development coaches in the United States.

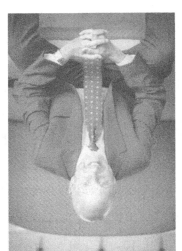

Tim is the author of *LeadWell-The Ten Competencies of Outstanding Leadership* and *Beyond Engagement*, high impact books about leading the right way and creating an organizational culture that is both healthy and successful. His works have been featured in many business and professional development publications.

Stylistically, Tim brings unparalleled commitment and enthusiasm to each engagement and works hard to make sure all participants not only learn but have fun along the way.

Personally, Tim makes his home in Las Vegas, Nevada with his fiancé Lynn, Zach and Nalah the rescue kittens and Sydney the Corgi. He is the father of two grown boys, continues a life-long love affair by playing men's league baseball and enjoys any outdoor adventure.

Please consider purchasing and reading:

A Heart for Leadership Journal and Workbook

LeadWell-The Ten Competencies of Outstanding Leadership

Beyond Engagement-Moving Your Organization to Full Health and High Performance

Available at **www.discoverAegis.com** or **www.heartforleadership.com**

or anywhere books are sold.

@DiscoverAegis
@HeartofLeaders

@DiscoverAegis

Made in the USA
Middletown, DE
21 August 2020